D1029220

Up the Line

A Celebration of Britain's Preserved Steam Railways

Geoff Swaine

The Crowood Press

First published in 2000 by
The Crowood Press Ltd
Ramsbury, Marlborough
Wiltshire SN8 2HR

© Geoff Swaine 2000

All rights reserved. No part of this publication may be reproduced or transmitted in any form or by any means, electronic or mechanical, including photocopy, recording, or any information storage and retrieval system, without permission in writing from the publishers.

British Library Cataloguing-in-Publication Data
A catalogue record for this book is available from the British Library.

ISBN 1 86126 345 7

All photographs by the author.

Edited, designed and typeset by Focus Publishing

Printed and Bound in China by Dah Hua Printing Press Co. Ltd.

Contents

Foreword 5

Introduction 6

1   North Norfolk Railway 8

2   Keighley and Worth Valley Railway 14

3   Bluebell Railway 22

4   West Somerset Railway 28

5   Nene Valley Railway 34

6   Llangollen Railway 40

7   Mid-Hants Railway 48

8   Swanage Railway 54

9   North York Moors Railway 60

10 East Lancs Railway 68

11 Severn Valley Railway 74

12 South Devon Railway 80

13 Paignton and Dartmouth Steam Railway 86

14 Great Central Railway 92

15 Kent and East Sussex Railway 100

16 Bo'ness and Kinneil Railway 106

17 Gloucestershire Warwickshire Railway 114

18 Buckingham Railway Centre 120

19 Isle of Wight Steam Railway 124

20 Midland Railway Centre 130

21 Didcot Railway Centre 136

22 Lakeside and Haverthwaite Railway 142

Appendix I   Thanks Dai 146

Appendix II   Prelude to Preservation 149

Appendix III   Wheel Arrangements 150

Appendix IV   Steam Guide 151

Index 158

Foreword

by Hon, Sir William McAlpine, Bt.

We are now half a century into railway preservation, from the early days of the Welsh narrow gauge railways. Followed, of course, by the great band of people who would not just stand by and watch the steam engines disappear without doing something about it.

Only an extreme optimist would then have predicted the part that these and later preservations would play in shaping Britain's transport heritage. So good a job have they made of it that it is no wonder that the present Rail and Local Authorities are looking at the locations with envy. Financial incentives are being offered to some to share the amenities for commuter, park and ride and freight use.

It is also good to see so many steam rail-tours happening on the main line which adds another dimension to the industry.

I, like many others, stand in awe at the sight of these magnificently turned out engines, and admire the dedication of all the volunteers who run the railways.

It gives me great pleasure to endorse a book on such a great subject, and to the author who was a one-time colleague of mine.

Bill McAlpine

Hon, Sir William McAlpine, Bt.

A favourite location for tourists and photographers alike. On the Llangollen railway right beside the A5, the Pannier tank engine No. 7754 takes a scheduled train out of Berwyn Station while still climbing the steep incline.

Introduction

In 1968, the last steam train ran in British Railways service. Well before this, groups of people had begun to get together to see if they could salvage anything of the transport system they loved.

The success of the narrow-gauge trains in Wales and the pioneering of the Middleton and Bluebell Railways gave them hope. After the infamous Beeching Report, which closed so many of the under-used branch lines in the early 1960s, British Railways was in the full flow of modernization. Its main objective was to replace all steam locomotives with either diesel or electric traction.

In the early days, those enthusiasts had a very difficult task in persuading BR to consider keeping lines open. BR's sole objective was to clear and strip the unwanted lines as quickly as possible, and remove the steam locos to the breakers' yards. However, towards the end of the decade, the enthusiasts' determination not to let steam die began to reap rewards. BR's attitude mellowed, and they started to give assistance to the many preservation societies whose sights were set on finding suitable lines for running preserved railways.

The difficulties facing the preservation societies were enormous. In most cases, tracks had been lifted, and anything saleable had been sold. Engines and rolling stock were not easy to come by. It was mainly thanks to the stockpile at Woodham Brothers yard at Barry, South Wales, that there was any supply at all.

Fortunately, the owners there had not broken up the couple of hundred rotting engines that they had purchased for scrap.

Sacrifice and fund raising were the name of the game. Leases on the buildings and trackbed had to be bought, together with all materials and equipment. In addition to this, a considerable amount of work had to be put in, in order to renovate that equipment, lay tracks, erect fencing, build workshops, and so on, and the stock had to be restored to working order.

Obviously, with the safety of passengers involved, Government departments were keeping a close eye on the work. Very high standards had to be met before a Light Railway Order was granted.

This book sets out to show how the different railways have progressed, and what they have achieved. It is a great success story. So many have tried, and almost all of them have succeeded. Many are at the end of their expansion possibilities, while others still have some way to go. New generations are hooked, and involved. Young children are smelling a smoky engine for the first time at 'Thomas' events. In years to come, they will bring their own children. Some of the lines can now afford to employ a few paid staff, but volunteers are still the backbone of the business, working unpaid, solely for the love of the steam engine.

In 1995, there was a new turn of events,

with the fiftieth anniversary of the end of the war. The preserved railways were able to put on some very special shows to commemorate the VE and VJ 50 anniversaries. It was a great opportunity for all concerned to transform the old stations and engines back to their wartime guises. Since that time, war themes have caught on in a big way, and are a regular feature of the seasonal programmes. Visitors play their part by dressing up in period costume.

The preserved railways need a continuous flow of young people to offer their skills. Anyone looking for friendly people should simply go into their favourite steam centre and ask, 'Can I help?' Older people who have time on their hands have a lifetime of experience to offer. They might derive much satisfaction from managing a station, for example, thereby helping to run a living steam museum and contributing to Britain's heritage.

Nowadays, the railways are complex business operations. With some seven million people visiting the centres every year, groups of enthusiasts can no longer run the railways solely as preservation societies. Thankfully, a number of people experienced in such industries as finance and leisure, and even the big railway, have become directors, many of them offering their services unpaid. Planning is a major task for them. Funds may only be diverted into new projects after the running of the railway has been looked after.

Present-day leisure seekers expect the best facilities, and are not impressed with such things as Edwardian earthenware lavatories. Enthusiasts expect an imaginative show, and many others come for different reasons: to take photographs, to be photographed, or to make tape recordings, and so on. Older enthusiasts like to see complete authenticity, so that they may re-live their own memories of the steam age.

The volunteers who have put in so many hours of work can have the satisfaction of knowing that their end product may last for just as long as the original railway. To save something is practically as good as building it in the first place.

Looking towards the future, many of the railways are now finding that they have a part to play in the community as well as being a tourist attraction. Some, like the East Lancs Railway, have made such an impact that the whole area has become revitalised. A formerly depressed area has benefited from the railway's influx of visitors. This sort of success gets noticed, and encourages local authorities elsewhere to give the utmost assistance to their local line. Some have helped generate park-and-ride schemes, while others have studied the possibility of lines with a town-centre station providing a service for commuters. The future for Britain's heritage railways looks very good.

This seems a good place to thank all those volunteers who have put in so much time. Many from the early days will be bowing out, and handing over to a new generation. There is still much to do and much to continue.

I would also like to thank all the people who have helped me during my trips around the country.

Apologies to the railways that I have not been able to include. To have added any more would have meant a general reduction in content for each chapter, and this would have changed the whole scope of the book.

Geoff Swaine

CHAPTER ONE

North Norfolk Railway

It would be easy to assume that the North Norfolk Railway line, being in East Anglia, would be situated in a rather flat landscape. Nothing could be further from the truth.

The 'Poppy Line' travels through a designated 'Area of Outstanding Natural Beauty'. Starting at the old station of Sheringham, beside the market in the heart of the town, the line rises up beside the coastal golf links, then turns inland through hilly heath and woodland, on its 5½ mile (9km) journey to the new station on the outskirts of Holt. Past somersault signals, the train arrives at Weybourne. The station still retains all its old-world charm from its days on the Midland and Great Northern Joint Railway. Passengers may stop off to inspect the railway's stockyard,

or the traditional signal box, before travelling on to Holt, via Kelling Camp Halt.

At Holt, the 'Holt Flyer' would have been a welcome sight to arriving travellers in the past. These horse-drawn buses were once a common sight around the town and village stations of Britain. As often as not in rural areas, the local station would be situated a mile or so out of the town or village. In the early days of railway expansion, the locals did not want the steam railway too close to their houses.

Constructed in 1887 for the Eastern and Midlands Railway, the North Norfolk Railway line was originated largely to promote tourism to this part of East Anglia. At first, the end of the line was Cromer, but, with amalgamations, there were soon connections from the Midlands to Great Yarmouth and Lowestoft. The NNR still harbours ambitions to reclaim and reopen the section of railway between Sheringham and Cromer. This section of line is still used by Regional Railways, with diesel 'Sprinter' DMUs operating.

Pride of the NNR now is the wonderfully restored green B12 engine. Formerly BR engine No. 61572 4-6-0, this engine underwent restoration in Germany for three-and-a-half years. Apart from a few outings in the late 1970s, it had been in mothballs since it was saved from destruction in 1962. On 4 March 1995, the restored B12 made its first passenger runs. Before this date, the railway had been running mainly with a Hunslet Austerity tank, and a borrowed 'Jinty', together with visiting locomotives from

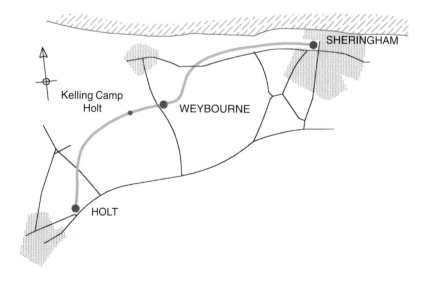

other railways for special occasions. It has now also built up a good selection of diesel engines, diesel car units, and rolling stock, including two former Brighton Belle Pullman Units. There is also an LNER Gresley Buffet Car, which has been restored to its original 1937 condition.

Closed by BR in 1964, the line was reopened by the Midlands and Great Northern Joint Railway Society in 1975, and has run successfully ever since. Now, with the B12, it is attracting nationwide attention. Other railways are queuing up to borrow the engine, offering their best stock in return.

The M&GN, along with the Somerset and Dorset Joint Railway, and a very few others, was able to keep its identity after the Grouping of 1923. Affectionately known as the 'Muddle and Get Nowhere' by its users, it was a typically sleepy line of the time. The present NNR is the Melton Constable to Cromer Beach branch of a railway that once

Snow is still on the ground from the day before, but the B12 has a sunny day for its first public outing on 4 March 1995; here it is seen arriving at Holt.

spanned five counties. Across country to Peterborough and beyond, that railway largely operated as a single-track mainline (again, like the Somerset and Dorset).

Restoration of the B12

No. 8572 is the only survivor of a class of ten locomotives built in 1928 for the LNER, and the only inside-cylinder 4-6-0 of any class to be saved for preservation. After 1948, it became BR Eastern Region No. 61572.

The engine was withdrawn from BR service in 1961, and sidelined until 1963 when, incredibly, it was steamed up again for a 'steam special' from London's Broad Street Station to Stratford-upon-Avon.

Credit for keeping the B12 away from the hands of the salvage companies has to go to former Norwich shedmaster Bill Harvey. Harvey hid away the locomotive long enough

for it to be directed towards preservation. He also led a team of enthusiasts in the 1980s in the quest for No. 61572's mechanical restoration.

Until its re-launch in 1995, the B12's life in preservation had been that of the sad bridesmaid, never the bride, always coming second in the priorities of the railway (after all, tracks and stations had to come first). It also used twice as much coal as the regular tank engines, which, in cash-strapped times, ensured its relegation to static display. The project of restoration never really got off the ground.

In the late 1970s, an appeal fund was set up. It was successful in getting work started, but this was spasmodic. In 1981, the boiler was re-tubed, but this work was later condemned, as it turned out not to be to the satisfaction of the BR inspectors, who could not see the inside of the boiler.

Work had to stop again, until Bill Harvey

A view from the Church Street bridge showing 3807 'Ring Haw' at the front of the next scheduled service. Alongside is the front of the former Southern Railway Brighton Belle Pullman.

The German built four-wheeled diesel car was thought to be the answer for Britain's branch lines in the 1950s. Here the little railcar leaves Weybourne with an off-peak service to Sheringham.

was able to organize a team to get the engine into a workable condition. Even if it was not going to be to mainline standards, they felt sure that they could get it into passable condition for running on the preserved line. Again, the project was dogged by bad luck. Although Bill Harvey's team restored the frame to working condition, the firm to whom the boiler was sent for refurbishment went into liquidation. This was a time of severe recession, and a second company was also unable to complete the work, although they did prove that the tubes that had been installed in 1981 did need to come out.

A decision was taken to send the locomotive to the Dutch firm of Brabantrail Brexon for complete restoration. Although the operation did not go completely smoothly, it was to prove successful in the end. The Dutch firm decided to send the frame and wheels to one of its offshoots in Kloster

Mansfeld, in the former East Germany. The boiler and firebox remained in the Netherlands, but Brabantrail Brexon soon found itself going into liquidation, and the boiler went into the hands of the receiver. Roger Heasman, who became the NNR Chief Engineer in 1991, was overseeing the proceedings, and couldn't help feeling that there was a jinx on the B12. He managed to persuade the new management of the Kloster Mansfeld works to finish the project. The boiler was moved there, and was reunited with the frame in late 1993.

It was to be another frustrating year before the restored locomotive returned to Norfolk. This gave the NNR's staff just twelve very busy weeks to get it ready for its well-publicized first outing, in March 1995. In addition, the drivers, firemen and mainten-ance staff had to be trained; after all, up to that point, they had only been operating tank engines.

'Ring Haw', the powerful little Hunslet Austerity engine, on its long climb to Weybourne Station.

0-6-0T 3809 Hunslet Austerity 'Ring Haw' attacks the 1 in 97 gradient out of Sheringham.

Above:
The Andrew Barclay 0-6-0T No. 100 (formerly 2107) in the M&GN livery of yellow ochre.

Below and right: **The long awaited first running in preservation of the unique restored B12. At 11:15am on 4 March 1995 the train arrives at Weybourne Station to be greeted by an assortment of enthusiasts and photographers.**

Below right:
The ex-LNER Gresley teak-bodied dining car; pride of the NNR coaching stock.

The ever faithful Hunslet Austerity No. 3809 'Ring Haw' crosses the bridge over the A149 between Sheringham and Weybourne.

Smoke is seen a mile away from Weybourne Station as No. 8572 approaches. It is fifteen minutes late on its first outing, admiration and excitement are felt by all at Weybourne.

The 'Holt Flyer' taking passengers from the new station of Holt down the long road to the town centre, a privately run service by The Railway pub in Holt.

After overhaul at the Malowa works in Germany, the LNER inside-cylindered 4-6-0 No. 8572 stands at Weybourne with a return train from Holt. Unique in preservation, it is proudly back in service after more than three decades, after being bought by the M&GN Society.

CHAPTER TWO

Keighley and Worth Valley Railway

The K&WVR Preservation Society has preserved a unique Midland Railway branch line, the only complete line in Britain to have been saved.

In its first twenty-five years of operation, the line, together with buildings and fittings, and some thirty locomotives, has been restored to the highest order. The line, with its vintage rolling stock, and authentic stations, which have gas and oil lighting, provides the complete Edwardian branch-line experience. Its restoration has led to the railway winning many awards.

During an enthusiasts' weekend, there will be up to six steam engines operating on one day, in a variety of formations. It is quite a sight to see two big engines double-heading a train down the valley. Sometimes, the vintage rolling stock may be wheeled out of the museum for a nostalgic run. There are splendid views of the line to be had from the hillside roadways, and a vintage bus is often provided by the railway for this purpose.

It is no surprise that the line has been in great demand for film and television use. Keighley Station was used for the evacuation scenes in the film *Yanks*, with the station being completely taken over for a whole week. Many other productions have been made here, including the television and film versions of *The Railway Children*, both starring Jenny Agutter.

The line begins at Keighley, which adjoins and connects with the Metro-Train line. This is part of the Leeds to Settle and Carlisle line, the most popular line in the country for steam workings. Many of the K&WVR locos have been involved in these steam adventures.

At Keighley, visitors can see the turntable,

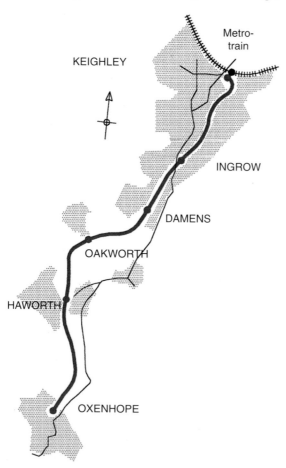

and watch the big engines being watered, and then backed on to the trains. The branch line curves to the right out of the station, then begins its 5½ mile (9km) trip down the valley.

After a climb up a tough gradient, the first stop is Ingrow, the home of the Vintage Carriage Trust Museum, which is situated beside the line. Ingrow's station building was moved brick by brick from a disused railway in Lancashire, and then expertly rebuilt. It has distinctive Midland Railway oil lamps on the platform. All the other stations down the line have gas lamps.

After leaving Ingrow, the trains steam on through a short tunnel, follow the river past old mill buildings, and arrive next at the tiny station of Damens. Trains only occasionally stop here because the platform is too short to accommodate more than one carriage. The station has marvellous gardens, which are maintained, as at all the stations, by volunteers. They are a real reminder of the dedication of times gone by.

The next stop is the Railway Children station of Oakworth, which has retained all its Edwardian charm. Original artefacts adorn the platform, including milkchurns, luggage and even a coffin trolley, reminding visitors that at one time virtually everything had to be moved by rail.

Haworth is the town of the Bronte family. All their literary works, including Emily's *Wuthering Heights*, can be bought at the station bookshop. On the platform, the

Former L&NWR Coal Tank 0-6-2 No. 1054 (built in 1888 at Crewe) waits at Ingrow to run with the evening branch-line special.

Stanier Jubilee Class 4-6-0 No. 45596 'Bahamas' in BR Brunswick green livery, standing at Keighley. The engine first entered service in 1934 after being built at the Queens Park Works, Scotland. No. 45596 had its double chimney fitted in 1960.

station staff are in immaculate uniforms. They operate the perfectly restored 'finger boards', which inform passengers of the next train. Haworth is the site of the railways headquarters, and the engine shed. A visit there in the early morning or late afternoon provides the opportunity to see volunteers at work on the engines.

The line between Haworth and Oxenhope passes through beautiful Pennine scenery. After a mill and a packhorse bridge, it leaves the river for the final stretch to the end of the line at Oxenhope. Just before reaching Oxenhope, on the right-hand side of the line, are Three Chimneys and Top Field. Here, many of the external scenes for the *Railway Children* were filmed.

Haydock Foundry 0-6-0 'Bellerophon'

'Bellerophon' is an outstanding example of how to preserve and exhibit a locomotive of historic interest.

'Bellerophon' was donated to the K&WVR Preservation Society by the NCB in 1966. Given the fact that it had had a working life of ninety years, and that all other Haydock engines had been cut up, much thought and effort went into the welfare of this important locomotive.

The NCB could only have used 'Bellerophon' as a static display, but it has now been brought back to life, and has been on many working tours around the preservation sites of Britain. It has turned out to be a triumph for the living museum. This is surely preservation at its best.

The LMS 8F and WD 2-8-0

The 8Fs were produced by William Stanier in 1935 for the LMS. They proved to be so successful that in 1939 the Ministry of Supply adopted them as the definitive freight engine for war use. From that time onwards, 8Fs were to be built in the workshops of all the big four railway companies. The number built finally amounted to some 850 examples, of which 300 were initially earmarked for overseas use. Many ended up on the ocean floor due to enemy action.

After the war, the 663 surviving engines were taken into British Railways service. Many of these continued right up to the 'end of steam' in 1968, with a good selection going into preservation.

The demand for heavy locomotives grew with the war effort, and in 1942 a cheaper austerity version of the 8F – the WD 2-8-0 – was ordered. This was expected to have a useful life of just two years leading up to the expected invasion of the Continent by the Allied forces.

In the end, 935 WD 2-8-0s were built. They proved to be so successful that, after the war, 733 were sold on to BR. Many lasted the course, but most became so dilapidated that they could not be saved by preservationists. One example, however, was rescued from Sweden by the Keighley and Worth Valley Railway. It is now the only survivor of the class, and has been fully restored to match the contingent that served British Railways.

The unmistakable stripped-down lines of a Josiah Evans, Foundry 0-6-0 tank engine.

BR Standard Class 4 No. 75078, together with 78022, about to return to the shed after performing a double-headed run.

Stanier 8F 2-8-0 No. 48431, working hard out of Keighley, and about to make short work of the 1 in 58 climb to Ingrow.

Above: **The ex-North Staffordshire Railway Class 4, 0-6-0 No. 4422 waits at the Haworth shed while 8F No. 48431 moves away to go into service.**

Left: **Departing from Ingrow with the branch-line special, Coal Tank 1054 gets set to take the train away with its vintage Metropolitan high-capacity suburban coaches.**

Plaque from the side of ex-Haydock Foundry locomotive 'Bellerophon'.

The low-tech image at Haworth, with gas lamps and immaculate station signage.

BR Standard Class 2 No. 78022 runs out of Keighley Station after a turn of duty.

Historic stove-enamelled advertising adorning the side of Oakworth Station.

A reminder that the railways used to have a duty as the common carrier. Here at Oakworth a coffin trolley stands on the platform.

The LMS 4-6-0 'Jubilee'

The 'Jubilee' was developed from the inefficient Claughtons and 'Baby Scots' by William Stanier, who was given the job of producing a much-needed engine for mid-range passenger express services. He based his design on the GWR four-cylinder Castle Class, following his experience at Swindon, where he had been Number Two to Charles Collett.

Early models were not without their problems. However, after necessary adjustments had been made to suit the 'Jubilee's three-cylinder motion, the class went on to be popular and long-lasting. The engine was very distinctive, with its tapered boiler and huge 6ft 9in wheels. The first of a total of 191 appeared in 1934, named in commemoration of the forthcoming Silver Jubilee of King George V, and given a special black and chrome livery. The rest were named mainly after military achievements and British territories abroad.

The distinctive three-cylinder motion gives three exhaust beats (chuffs) to each revolution of the driving wheels. It is a very basic and gratifying sound, which has helped endear this engine to a large army of Midlands spotters.

Only four examples remain: No. 45593 'Kolhapur', No. 45596 'Bahamas', No. 45690 'Leander', and No. 45699 'Galatea'.

CARRIAGE MUSEUM

The earliest engine thought to have outside cylinder motion that is still working – the ex-Haydock Foundry engine 'Bellerophon', here taking part in an enthusiasts' working.

Below: **Early morning activity at the Haworth Shed. Being prepared for the day's work are BS 4MT No. 75078, 8F No. 48431, Pannier tank No. 5775, and a class 20 diesel.**

Above: **The ex-L&NWR Coal Tank being wheeled out of the Ingrow Museum to take part in the enthusiasts' day.**

CHAPTER THREE

Bluebell Railway

The Bluebell and the Middleton Railways were the first standard-gauge preserved railways in Britain. The Bluebell opened in August 1960, after closure of the line by British Railways two years earlier, and became the pacesetter for all the rest to follow.

BR's closure of the line generated much publicity. Due to incorrect procedure, the first attempt failed, and the line stayed open. Ultimately, it did close, but by then a few students had picked up on the idea of preserving it. Inspired by the success of the Welsh narrow-gauge railways, a preservation society of some strength was formed, and deputations were made to British Railways.

The society was successful in saving the line, but was only able to obtain a leasehold on the section south of Horsted Keynes. BR was still using the Haywards Heath to Horsted Keynes branch for freight.

The original railway opened in 1876, and ran from East Grinstead to Lewes. The Bluebell Railway Preservation Society had been able to save just 2½ miles (4km) of it in the middle of the countryside, but it was a start. The story of the Bluebell Railway was to become one of the great success stories of railway preservation.

In the beginning, two tank engines were obtained: Stroudley Terrier No. 32655 'Stepney', and former SE&CR No. 31323. Together with just two coaches, these were all that the society possessed.

A temporary station needed to be built at Horsted Keynes, but there was no room to have a 'runaround' facility for the engine. The only way a train could operate was to have an engine at each end. This situation continued until the line from Haywards Heath was finally closed, in October 1963. BR lifted all the track, as well as the disused track north of Horsted Keynes. (The section south of Sheffield Park had been removed in 1959.)

The Bluebell Railway was now very much

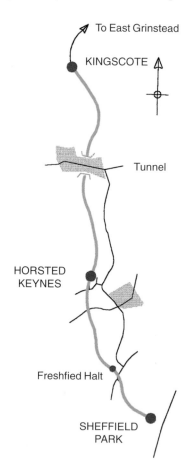

To East Grinstead

KINGSCOTE

Tunnel

HORSTED KEYNES

Freshfied Halt

SHEFFIELD PARK

The pioneer train is recreated for a special running between Sheffield Park and Horstead Keynes. There is an engine at both ends of the train, and here SECR loco No. 323 heads into Sheffield Park.

on its own, but it was able to take over full use of Horsted Keynes Station. This meant that it could have 'runaround' facilities at both ends of the line, and trains could finally run with a single engine.

The society never stopped being ambitious. It gradually overcame problems in purchasing the freehold, then it built up stocks of engines and rolling stock for restoration, together with further acquisitions of land. Covered accommodation and workshops were built at Horsted Keynes and Sheffield Park.

A second phase of locomotive works was also started at Sheffield Park in 1979. A new locomotive shed meant that a large number of locomotives could be housed under cover. In

1986, also at Sheffield Park, the buffet and restaurant facility was built.

Gradually, the line has been extended towards the place that had always been its objective – East Grinstead. By April 1992, it had reached, and passed, Sharpthorne Tunnel, the longest double-bore tunnel on any British preserved line. In 1994, it reached Kingscote. Planning permission was obtained to make the final run into East Grinstead Station, and achieve a connection with the Railtrack network.

All lines near to a main line aim to get a connection with it. It is most useful for stock movements, and for the running of special excursions. However, running a preserved

No. 263 H Class 0-4-4T, built at the Ashford works in 1905.

British Standard 9Fs

Of all the British Standard Classes introduced in the 1950s, the 9Fs were the most numerous, with 251 examples being built – 198 at Crewe, and 53 at Swindon. Included with the Swindon batch was the last BR steam engine ever to be produced, No. 92220 'Evening Star'. Another was purchased by David Shepherd, and was later named 'Black Prince'. Only one other, No. 92203, was preserved direct from BR. In years to come, another seven were saved from the Barry scrapyard, including No. 92240.

The design of the class owes something to the War Department 2-10-0 Class (*see* North York Moors Railway), both being designed by R.A. Riddles. The ten driving wheels have flangeless centre wheels, to assist the loco's curve-taking ability.

Built for heavy freight traffic, the 9Fs were also very useful for passenger work on severe routes. They were particularly well known for hauling the 'Pines Express' on the Somerset and Dorset Joint Railway.

Despite having relatively small driving wheels, the 9Fs had a sharp turn of speed, and it was not unknown for them to exceed 80mph (130km/h).

line into a mainline station, and using its facilities, can be an expensive business, as the South Devon Railway has found to its cost. A separate terminus is much to be preferred. The Bluebell Railway has a site adjacent to East Grinstead Station, which they intend to adopt.

The Bluebell's interchange with the mainline station will attract large numbers of new customers. One of the Bluebell Railway's long-standing problems has been its inaccessibility to non-car users, although a vintage Routemaster bus has been used for many years to take visitors from East Grinstead to Kingscote.

The final stage of development of the Bluebell Railway is not without major problems. Several parts of the trackbed are in different ownerships; a cutting has been filled with refuse and has to be cleared; a ten-arch viaduct needs remedial work; and a new terminus will need to be built. A very smart and imaginative Art Deco design has been favoured, which will be something unique to the preservation movement.

Left: **British Standard 9F No. 92240 in preparation for duty at Sheffield Park.**

Above: **The boiler and firebox of a British Standard 2 loco, undergoing restoration at Sheffield Park.**

The year 2000 marks the railway's fortieth anniversary. A look around the complex at Sheffield Park shows how much has been achieved. Its collection of over thirty locomotives, most of which are operational, and beautifully turned out. It is not unusual to see up to ten in steam on a special occasion; this gives an indication of the volunteer base that the railway enjoys.

The fine South Eastern and Chatham livery is seen in all its glory on Nos. 263 and 592. Both these locomotives have now been joined by newly restored Stirling 01 Class No. 65. The Bluebell Railway can now put on a lavish SECR spectacular with these magnificent engines.

The Southern Railway was only in existence for twenty-five years. In that time, it had only two Chief Mechanical Engineers: R.E.L. Maunsell and the extrovert O.V. Bulleid. Maunsell developed such classes as the School and the King Arthur, together with other superbly engineered locos of traditional design. Bulleid was more of an innovator and broke the mould with the introduction of the air-smoothed Merchant Navy Class (*see* Swanage Railway, pages 54–59). When he was asked to provide a war-time austerity loco, Bulleid came up with the ugly-duckling Q Class.

The Sheffield Park signal cabin is located right on the platform, and all the old levers and code machines are operational. On the far side is the electrically operated token-release machine for single-line working.

The driving wheels and complicated piston area of the 9F shows the extent of technical expertise that is required in the restoration of a locomotive.

O.C. Bulleid's Q1 Class 0-6-0 No. C1, on loan from the National Collection.

9F No. 92240 2-10-0 leaving Horsted Keynes with a northbound train. Purchased in 1978 from the Barry scrapyard in South Wales, the engine did not run in steam again until 1990, twenty-five years after being scrapped by BR, which had only used it for seven years in service.

No. C1 runs around the train at Sheffield Park.

The friendly little machines that served the public in the 1930s, a 'Black Cat' cigarette machine and the Nestlés chocolate machine.

On a regular service, S15 Class 4-6-0 No. 847 is delayed at Sheffield Park waiting for the return of the special running of the Pioneer train.

Above: **The Pioneer approaching Horsted Keynes, with SECR No. 263 at the head.**

Below: **SECR Loco No. 263 in authentic green forms one end of the Pioneer train.**

CHAPTER FOUR

West Somerset Railway

Without anybody really noticing, this line has been extended and built into one of Britain's leading preserved railways. At present it is the longest, covering 18 miles (29km), from Minehead to Bishops Lydeard. A further 2 miles (3km) to Taunton are in place, where it also has the prized possession of a connection to the Railtrack network. These last two miles are

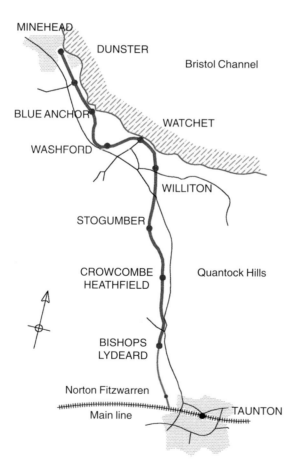

used only for special occasions, and stock movements. The track passes through the grounds of a cider company, and at present only limited workings are practical. There are also the costs of using the Railtrack lines to be considered before a service into Taunton can be established.

The West Somerset Railway has had some problems with expanding so fast. Its finances were stretched to the limit, and the railway has been on the brink of insolvency. For a long time it was only able to run one steam train on the line at a time. With such a long line, a round trip was taking over two hours. It was not the sort of service that the public wanted. However, with the growth in interest in steam preservation, the situation was turned around to produce, what is now, a major tourist attraction.

Closed by British Railways in 1971, the line was opened just five years later by the preservationists. Their endeavour and ambition have made it what it is today.

Bishops Lydeard is effectively the terminus at the Taunton end. There are excellent facilities here for visitors, including a Visitor Centre, with a museum that can house a full-sized engine, and has working signal displays.

As well as the Great Western Railway, the former Somerset and Dorset Joint Railway is well represented, although it did not actually run over the preserved line. The S&D ran from nearby Burnham and Bridgwater right through to Bournemouth, picking up a line from Bath at Evercreech Junction. Washford, one of the stations along the West Somerset Railway line,

The distinctive cab area of No. 71000.

British Standard Class 71000 'Duke of Gloucester' stands behind the S&D No. 88 at Minehead.

has been dedicated to the S&D. Among its displays are rolling stock, and a replica of the signal cabin from Midford Station, near Bath. Pride of place among the S&D exhibits goes to the working SDJR Fowler locomotive 2-8-0. Built in 1925 for heavy freight, it was well suited to the severe nature of the former railway.

Williton Station is the passing place for trains on most of the West Somerset Railway's timetables. It is also the home of the Diesel and Electric Preservation Group. This group has rebuilt many diesel locomotives, and these regularly run on the line. Diesels have a very special following, and are an essential part of all preserved railways.

The West Somerset Railway line begins at the popular seaside resort of Minehead. The station has one of the best locations a railway could wish for – right in the heart

---

History Note – The Somerset and Dorset Joint Railway

The Somerset and Dorset Joint Railway was formed in 1862 with the amalgamation of two local railway companies. They merged to provide a rail link from the Bristol Channel to the English Channel. From Bournemouth West the line stretched right across to Burnham, with branches to Bridgwater and Wells.

The station at Burnham was sited near the coast. There was an adjacent pier, from which coal trucks shipped over from Wales could be pulled up to the station by wire rope.

The extension to Bath was opened in 1874, starting from Evercreech Junction. The line passed through Shepton Mallet, and onwards and upwards over the Mendips, with the summit being at Masbury. It then went down to Radstock, crossing the Frome to the Bristol branch line, with the final section through Midford and down the notorious Devonshire Bank. Into Bath it linked with the Midland Railway (later the LMS), and shared the Bath Green Park Station.

The Midland Railway was happy to have a joint agreement with the S&D because it provided a link to the south coast. The premier passenger express train that ran from Manchester to Bournemouth and joined the S&D at Bath was the 'Pines Express'.

The Devonshire Bank was a notorious climb out of Bath for a steam engine. A banking engine (pushing from behind) was required for all but the lightest trains. At the top of the 1:50 incline were two tunnels. The trains were still working the climb while passing through the tunnels. It is hard to imagine now the appalling conditions the crew had to endure in the open cabs. The passengers would also have suffered, with smoke going into the carriages.

Some parts of the S&D were single-tracked and some were double. With the diversity of locomotives that served the line, the railway liked to be considered a main line. Passenger services, though, serving a sparsely populated area, were generally more typical of a sleepy branch line. Often, the engines would stop to deliver water or milk to a signalman and the driver would perhaps get a rabbit in return.

For the big climb over the Mendips, large engines were always on stand by to be added to the front of the trains as pilots. The heavy stone trains from the Mendip quarries especially needed these.

After its closure in 1966, the railway began to win more affection than it had before. (It had been considered by some to be the poor relation of the GWR.) This growth in popularity was largely due to Ivo Peters, who had photographed and filmed the railway extensively, and left a wealth of material. This aroused much interest over the years, and is now part of the Somerset and Dorset Museum Trust archive, based at Washford on the West Somerset Railway.

In its later years the railway featured some exciting locomotives. As well as some Standard Classes, including the great 9Fs, there were SR West Country Classes and MR Black Fives, as well as its own 2-8-0s.

The severe nature of the S&D route across the Mendips, and up the notorious Devonshire Bank out of Bath, demanded the use of the strongest engines. A typical example was the Fowler 7F No. 53808, built in 1925, especially for the heavy-freight workings of the S&D. Preserved by the S&D Railway Trust and based on the West Somerset Railway, the 7F can now be seen running with its original number, 88.

of the town, and on the sea front, it attracts visitors like a magnet. Workshops and an engine shed are located there, and there is always much to be seen outside. The station was built in 1874, at the height of the Victorian boom in seaside resort expansion. In BR days it was never as big as it is today. The preservation society has expanded it so that it can accommodate a full-length special excursion coming off the main line.

At all stations along the line the West Somerset Railway links with special attractions and tourist spots. Many are especially good stopping-off points for parents with children, who might find the whole journey rather on the long side.

The workings from the signal box at Midford station on the former Somerset and Dorset Joint Railway, have been re-housed in a replica signal box at Washford Station.

After running around the train at Bishops Lydeard, the Prairie No. 4160 (built after nationalization) joins the train with a very interested spectator.

The Henry Fowler 2-8-0 loco No. 88, built in 1925 for heavy mineral train working, standing outside the engine shed at Minehead.

An S&D signal cabin on the platform at Washford station, with fittings from the Midford station signal box on the old S&D Railway.

In the museum at Bishops Lydeard are the commemorative headboards for special trains which run on the line. The 'Taunton 150' board was for the 150 years of train services to Taunton celebrations.

The Fowler 2-8-0 No. 88 heading for Bishops Lydeard, about to cross the busy A358 Williton to Taunton road.

The 'Manor' Class is the ideal engine for use on Great Western preserved lines. Here, 'Odney Manor' (built by BR in 1950), its day's duty finished, stands outside the Minehead shed.

Making sure that everyone is looked after, the staff at Bishops Lydeard help some people with a chair lift.

A visitor for a summer season. Manor Class No. 7828 'Odney Manor' arrives at the long platform in Minehead, which was extended to accommodate full-length (fourteen-coach) trains coming off the main line on special excursions.

GWR Manor Class

The Manor Class was a Collett engine introduced in 1938 to a specification that would suit service on the 'light-loading' gauged lines of mid-Wales. It proved to be a very suitable engine for many cross-country services, and longer branch lines on the GWR network, and also became a favourite for hauling Royal trains.

Twenty examples of the class were introduced in 1938: Nos. 7800 to 7819. A further ten – Nos. 7820 to 7829 – were added by BR in 1950. Nine examples have survived into preservation. With their classic Great Western styling, they are proving to be one of the most popular engines to work on the preserved lines of the West Country, being perfectly suited for working all but the heaviest trains.

The successor to the Manor was the BR Standard Class 4 4-6-0, which was designed to cover the same areas of operation.

CHAPTER FIVE

Nene Valley Railway

In the late 1960s, the forward-thinking Peterborough Development Corporation proposed the establishment of a National Transport Museum in the city, to be run in conjunction with a preserved railway. In the end, however, the Government located the museum at York. In 1970, the Peterborough Locomotive Society was set up, and offered steam-driven goods-van rides in the grounds of the local sugar factory. In 1972, it became the Peterborough Railway Society, with the wider aim of forming a preserved steam line. The society was supported by the Development Corporation, and a scheme was developed to run the line through the 200-acre designated leisure complex of Nene Park.

The railway opened in 1974, a little later than other preserved railways, most of which were up and running by this time. The Nene Valley Railway experienced some difficulty in obtaining stock, the best of which had already been snapped up from the Woodham Brothers scrapyard at Barry, in South Wales, the only salvage dealer who had not cut up engines discarded by BR.

NVR's solution was to look abroad, where it found some success, and as a result the railway now has an identity that is completely different from that of any other. It has a collection of locomotives from Poland, France, Germany and Sweden, together with some British stock, and its ex-Polish State Railway locomotive No. 7173 is the largest engine in service on any British line.

This unusual stock-sourcing has given the railway a unique money-making edge over the others. It finds itself constantly in demand from film and television companies making productions that involve foreign railway scenes. Scenes from such major films as *Octopussy* and *The Dirty Dozen* have been shot here, and in 1995, a number of huge fire scenes for the James Bond spectacular *Goldeneye* were filmed at Castor Bridge.

NVR also has a very special 'Thomas the Tank Engine', which was named personally by the late Reverend W. Awdry, the originator of the *Thomas the Tank Engine* stories. In 1971, when the ex-Peterborough Sugar Factory engine Hudswell Clarke 0-6-0 No. 1800 was giving rides within the factory compound, the Reverend Awdry agreed to come to one of the open days, and christened the engine 'Thomas'.

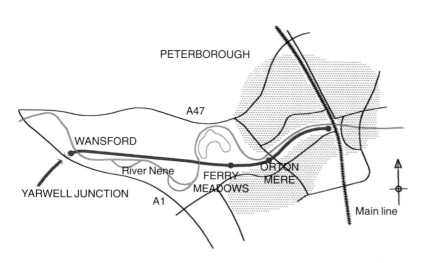

Wansford is the railways headquarters. Over the past twenty years, the station area has grown into a large complex, with railway buildings, sheds and sidings. It adjoins what used to be the old A1 Great North Road, the now diverted A1, which crossed the railway here. In the not-too-distant past, many a motorist would have been delayed at the Wansford level crossing. The crossing gates, and a huge sixty-frame signal box, built in 1907, remain. Also, at the end of the platform, are examples of Great Northern Railway somersault signals.

In June 1995, the line celebrated a very special event. Called the Peterborough 'Rail 150' Festival, it celebrated the 150th anniversary of the first train service to Peterborough. Star of the show was a special train hauled by 'Locomotion', a replica of the 1825 train. The celebrations continued with a big engine gala, featuring the most significant assembly of visiting steam locomotives ever to appear on the railway. They included 'Sir Nigel Gresley', 'The Great Marquess', 'Canadian Pacific' and 'Bahamas', all in steam, together with the huge Class 40 diesel locomotive D306.

Gala events and 'European' weekends are now regular features in the NVR calendar. Regularly now on show is the Battle of Britain Class No.

No. 3442 'The Great Marquess' 2-6-0 K4 Class, built especially for use on the Scottish West Highland route, from Glasgow to Fort William and Mallaig, where weight restrictions were in force. A powerful light engine was required, and six examples of the class were produced. Each had a Scottish name, such as 'Cameron of Locheil' and 'Lord of the Isles'. No. 3442 was built at Darlington in 1938, and spent all its working life in Scotland, until being withdrawn from service in 1961. From 1963 to 1967, 'The Great Marquess' worked many rail tours in the north-east of England before a steam ban was imposed by British Railways. The engine arrived at the Severn Valley Railway in 1972, and had limited use until the 1980s, when a major overhaul was undertaken. Since 1987, 'The Great Marquess' has been working regularly again, running rail tours, and being loaned to other preserved railways, including the Nene Valley Railway, where it spent the 1995 summer season.

The A4 Class

The A4 Class is the ultimate steam engine, with the style and performance to make the pulse race. Seeing one approaching, and hearing that distinctive siren, caused just as much excitement in the past as it does today. Designed by Sir Nigel Gresley, for the London to Edinburgh east-coast route, it is a fine sight at speed.

Production started at Doncaster in 1935, the year of the Silver Jubilee, and Gresley had the first four examples kitted out in a special silver-grey livery to commemorate the Royal occasion. They were used on the special London to Newcastle 'Silver Jubilee' train, advertised as Britain's first streamlined train.

Its huge driving wheels and streamlined shape helped make the A4 the fastest-running steam loco ever. No. 60022 (formerly LNER 4468) 'Mallard' holds the world steam speed record of 126mph (202km/h), achieved in 1938. 'Sir Nigel Gresley' shows a plaque on its side stating that it holds the post-war steam speed record of 112mph (180km/h), achieved in 1959. In all, thirty-four examples of the class were built, of which there are only four survivors.

This replica of an 1825-built locomotive is the star of the show at the Peterborough 150 festival, celebrating the 150th anniversary of the arrival of the railway to Peterborough. A re-enactment of the opening ceremony was performed with 'Locomotion'.

34081 '92 Squadron', which was renovated from 'Barry condition' by NVR volunteers. It is now resplendent in the original Bulleid livery of malachite green and yellow lining.

The railway has had a massive influence on the history and development of Peterborough. It was a great crossroads of lines, heavily used by passenger and freight traffic, and sited on the former Great Northern Railway, route of the great 'races to the north'. The line over which the NVR now runs was built in 1845, and became part of the former London and North Western Railway, with links to Birmingham. After the 1923 Grouping, it became part of the LMS.

History Note – The 'Races to the North'

Competition between the former private railway companies was intense. For those that operated between London and Scotland, it was an ongoing race to establish ever-decreasing journey times.

Before the coming of the railways the quickest way to get from London to Scotland was by sea. The innovation of the steam locomotive, running fast on tracks, changed people's lives for ever. It was exciting, romantic and inspirational, and the Victorians loved it. The competitive element led to the great 'races to the north', and the London-Edinburgh and London-Aberdeen runs became the 'Blue Ribands' of the railway services.

The west-coast route ran from London Euston via Crewe, Preston and Carlisle. The east-coast route ran from London King's Cross on the Great Northern route via Doncaster, York and Newcastle to Edinburgh. Then it went on across the Forth and Tay Bridges to head for Aberdeen.

Each route had the same London departure time. 10.00am for the Edinburgh run and 8.30am for Aberdeen. Both also had a night service to Aberdeen, leaving London at 8.00pm.

The key point on the Aberdeen run was Kinnaber Junction, 38 miles (61km) short of Aberdeen, where both lines converged on to one set of tracks. The first train to get signalled through the junction could not be beaten.

The main focus was on ever-decreasing journey times for the 400-mile (640-km) London to Edinburgh run. The achievements were extraordinary – the time was reduced from ten hours in 1869 to six hours in 1933, achieved by the 'Coronation Scot' on a southbound west-coast run.

From the late 1890s, the racing subsided, as it was taking its toll on man and machine. It was not until the new breeds of Gresley and Stanier locomotives came in that it was to start up again. Streamlining was all the rage in the 1930s, and the Coronations, Duchesses and A4s provided all the excitement.

The A1(3) Class engine 'Flying Scotsman' (which shares the name of the more famous train), made the first non-stop run in 1928. This was helped by the innovation of the walk-through tender, which allowed crews to be changed at the half-way point without the train stopping.

Locomotive No. 101A (Swedish State Railways No. 1697) crosses the yard at Wansford.

A hive of activity at the Nene Valley, with 60007 awaiting to depart from Wansford with a westbound train. On the other track a goods train passes through.

Clouds of steam rise as A4 No. 60007 pulls out of Wansford Station.

The rear of 'Sir Nigel Gresley''s tender, showing the corridor link from engine to train. This would enable the crew to be changed on a non-stop London to Edinburgh run.

German-built No. 64305 tank engine stands on the turntable at the Wansford site.

Battle of Britain Pacific No. 34081 '92 Squadron' about to cross the River Nene on its approach to Wansford.

No. 230D116 in the Wansford sidings. Before nationalization of the French Railways in 1938, the engine carried the number 3.628. Built in 1911 by the German builders Henschell & Co. for the Nord Railways of France, she worked right through to the mid 1960s. This loco had the privilege of working the very first train on the Nene Valley Railway on the 1 June 1977.

Front view of the Nord Railway loco No. 230D116 as she waits beside the platform at Wansford.

Battle of Britain locomotive 34081, heads a westbound train out of Wansford.

Continental engines on display at a Euro Day. In the foreground German 2-6-2T No. 64305, with the Swedish Class 5. 2-6-2T behind.

No.60007 about to depart Wansford during the Peterborough 150 festival.

The engine that was personally named 'Thomas' by the Rev. W. Awdry author of the Thomas books, in 1971. Built by Hudswell Clarke in 1947 the little engine had spent its earlier days working for the Peterborough Sugar Factory.

The German-built ex-Polish State Railways 2-10-0 No. 7173, the largest operational steam locomotive in Britain. The large loco does not get many outings these days, because of its high running costs.

One of the great stalwarts of preservation, visiting from the Severn Valley Railway, LNER K4 Class No. 3442 'The Great Marquess' leaves Wansford.

CHAPTER SIX

Llangollen Railway

The station at Llangollen is in a superb location. Right beside the River Dee, in the heart of the town, it provides endless fascination for its visitors. The old bridge across the river makes a fine viewing gallery.

The town is on the main A5 trunk road, just inside the Welsh border, and just 15 miles (25km) from Chester. It is very accessible, and a starting-off point for many tourists and holidaymakers to North Wales. As well as the steam railway, mountains, waterfalls, a canal and an aqueduct are among the attractions.

The railway was formerly the Flint and Deeside. A society was set up in 1972 to take over the completely run-down Llangollen Station, with the aim of re-creating the steam railway. Nine years later, on 26 July 1981, the first train ran, along to the former Pentrefelin sidings, just before the river crossing. (Llangollen Station had been reopened in

1975, with just sixty feet of track in place.)

The next target was Berwyn, which is in a particularly difficult – but beautiful – position, perched on a shelf half-way up a mountain. This was reached by the society in 1985, but not without difficulties. Volunteers carried out all the track clearance and line re-laying, but the necessary extensive repairs to the bridge over the River Dee were done by contractors. Various grants were received, and the work was carried out at a cost of £30,000. The section to Berwyn was completed in 1985, and passenger services started in 1986.

The incline climbing up the side of the mountain to Berwyn Station is one of the most exciting features of the line. This gradient has been measured at one in eighty, but some of the drivers suggest that it is closer to one in forty. Visitors might agree that the drivers have a point!

Fortunately, when the line was finally

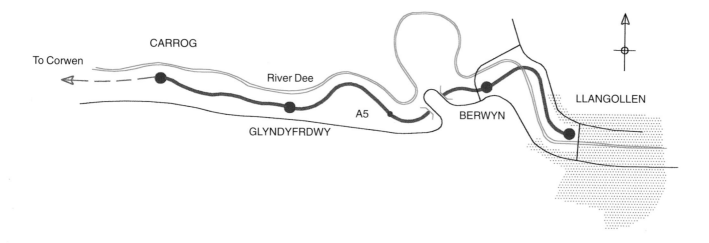

closed by British Railways in 1968, the local council had had the foresight to purchase Llangollen Station and the trackbed. This encouraged the enthusiasts who wanted the line reopened. As always, the authorities were obliged to ensure that the group was able to proceed, and that it would be safe for the public to be carried. The Department of Transport insists on a Light Railway Order, for which the requirements are very stringent, and progress can be slow. In 1981, with the railway up and running, the council granted the society a 21-year lease for the whole of the trackbed from Llangollen to Corwen, a distance of 10 miles (16km).

The 'Jinty' vs GWR 'Pannier' Tank

Two of the great tank engines from the former railway system oppose each other at the Llangollen Railway. The GWR 'Pannier' and the LMS 'Jinty' were the unsung workhorses of the railways, whether performing menial shunting duties, taking goods trains, or working branch-line or short-haul passenger services.

The 'Pannier' (generally known as the 5700 Class) has superior acceleration, can perform admirably with a rake of six coaches, and is especially good on hills. The 'Jinty' driver enthuses about the roomy cab and better vision, as well as the easier handling of the more classic LMS design.

No. 7822 'Foxcote Manor' at the new shed at Llangollen. The engine was rebuilt at the Llangollen Railway, and has since performed regularly on the line. Built at Swindon in 1949, it spent only fifteen years in BR service, working mostly on the Cambrian lines, often heading the Shrewsbury to Aberystwyth section of the 'Cambrian Coast Express'.

At the station, the travellers can have a good look and take some photographs. This is the view from the bridge at the end of the line at Llangollen.

Above: **'Flying Scotsman'**
Around every corner there is a surprise on a preserved railway. Standing in the shed area at Llangollen is the most famous of them all – the A3 Pacific No. 60103 'Flying Scotsman', fitted with German-style smoke deflectors. After a short spell on the railway in 1995, the ex-LNER loco developed a smoke leak from the firebox, and had to be taken out of service and returned to its Southall base to undergo a major overhaul.

Built in Doncaster, 'Flying Scotsman' hauled the first non-stop London to Edinburgh train in 1928, and in 1934 became the first locomotive officially to reach 100mph (160km/h). Taken out of service in 1963, the engine achieved international fame with trips to America and Australia.

After British Railways abolished steam in 1968, for a few years 'Flying Scotsman' was the only engine permitted to run over the main line with steam specials. For these it needed to run with two tenders, as all coal and watering facilities had been removed.

In July 1999, the famous engine made a spectacular comeback, with a commemorative run between London's King's Cross and Doncaster.

The stage from Berwyn to Glyndyfrdwy was completed in 1991, thanks largely to a grant from the Welsh Tourist Board. The reinstatement of the station at Glyndyfrdwy was not straightforward. The original building had become a private dwelling, and there was a children's playground on the trackbed. With cooperation all round, the problems were overcome. The level crossing was reinstated, and a signal box, which had formerly been at Leaton, near Shrewsbury, was brought in. By April 1992, the target had been reached.

The further extension to Carrog was achieved by 1999, only the final push to Corwen remains to complete the line.

The Llangollen Railway is another episode in the story of the enthusiast-volunteers who are seeing their dreams fulfilled, keeping steam engines running on the railways of Britain, which were abandoned in the 1960s.

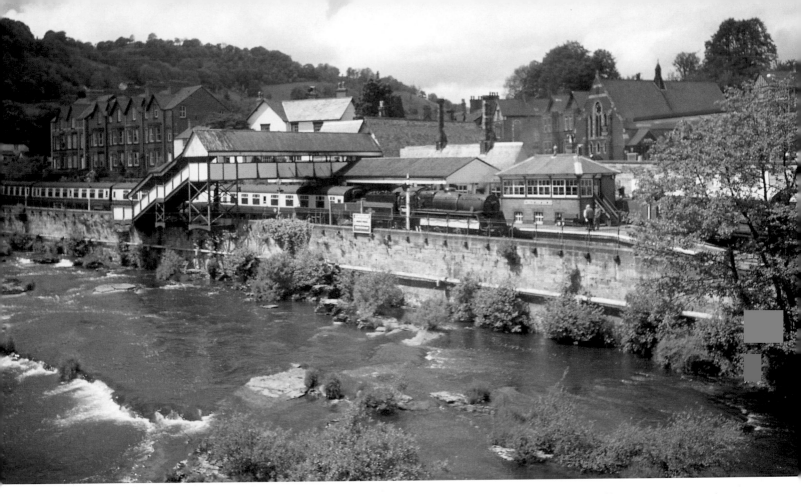

Above: **The grandstand view of Llangollen Station, from the old bridge, above the fast-running river. Cramped between the Abbey Road and the river, the station does not have much space to spare, but it is still a magnet for sightseers.**

Below: **Pannier tank No. 7754 about to depart from Berwyn Station.**

British Standard Types

After nationalization in 1948, the new British Railways executive embarked on an ambitious modernization programme. This was to build a new fleet of locomotives to suit all require-ments, from top express engines through to tank engines, and not forgetting a full range of mixed-traffic classes. They were to incorporate all up-to-date innovations and be easy to maintain. Many of the classes were designed to be direct replacements for types already in existence.

Twelve classes were finally built under the supervision of Robert Riddles, to provide this cross-section to suit all requirements. They were to be built at various depots all across the country.

At the top of the range there were three types of Pacific (4-6-2) designated for express passenger work. They were as follows:

1   the 70xxx Britannia (two-cylinder) Class (55 built);

2   the 71xxx (three-cylinder) Class, which ended up with just one example – No. 71000 'Duke of Gloucester';

3   for express passenger traffic only, the 72xxx 'Clan', a lighter version of the Britannia. Ten were built for Scottish use.

The ranges that followed these down the scale were as follows:

1   the 9F 92xxx 2-10-0 built for heavy freight (251 built);

2   73xxx Class 5, 4-6-0, designed to supersede the faithful 'Black Five' Class of the LMS (172 built). Nos. 73125-73154 had Caprotti valve-gear fitted;

3   75xxx Class 4, 4-6-0, lightweight, introduced to replace the 'Manor' of the GWR, with the mid-Wales routes in mind (80 built);

4   76xxx Class 4, 2-6-0, based on the heavier Ivatt Class 4 (115 built);

5   77xxx Class 3, 2-6-0, built for lightly laid routes (20 built);

6   78xxx Class 2, 2-6-0. Standard Ivatt Class 2 type (65 built);

7   80xxx Class 4, 2-6-4T, the trusty and well-liked Fowler/Stanier/Fairburn design continued (155 built);

8   82xxx Class 3, 2-6-2T, tank version of 77xxx type (45 built);

9   84xxx Class 2, 2-6-2T, based on Ivatt Class 2 tank (30 built).

In 1955, British Railways decided to make the profound decision to phase out all steam locomotion, in favour of diesel and electric traction. Standard classes which were under order continued to be produced, with the last coming out of production in 1960. This was 9F No. 92270 'Evening Star', built at Swindon. These later engines were to have a very short working life on BR.

Seen from the footbridge, No. 76079 in the process of slipping to the other end of the train.

'Jinty' No. 7298 waiting at Llangollen to take a train westbound. In recent times, No.7298 has been called upon to do some 'Thomas' duties.

The diminutive little 'Thomas' here trying his best with a full load on the Berwyn Bank. However, there is assistance behind in the shape of a Class 20 diesel. Up front, the engine is the much travelled J72 from the North York Moors railway, who in his former life would have had things a lot less hectic, somewhere in the north-east.

**Standard Class 4 No. 76079 'Castell Dinas Bran' at Llangollen station,
named after the ruined castle above the town.**

CHAPTER SEVEN

Mid-Hants Railway

This delightful railway, known as the 'Watercress Line', is a tribute to the enthusiast-volunteer, and a fine example of achievement. The line provides a service between Alresford and Alton via Ropley, for a distance of 10 miles (16km). It is a wonderful journey by steam, with the engines giving maximum effort up the gradients.

Formerly, the line was a quiet backwater of the Southern Railway, serving villages and country communities. Much of the watercress that grew in the extensive beds of the chalkstreams around Alresford, which gave the line its name, was transported by rail.

The line survived the Beeching closures, but was closed by British Railways a decade later, in 1973. It was reopened as a preserved line in April 1977, starting with the renovation of the station buildings at Alresford and Ropley, and the track between.

Grants had been obtained from the English Tourist Board and Hampshire County Council. The first rolling stock was delivered in March 1976, via Alton. Shortly after this, the track between Alton and Ropley was lifted by BR. The track had not been part of the society's purchase, although the trackbed of this section had been.

The original line was opened in 1865 as part of the Mid-Hants Railway. It was operated by the L&SWR, as a cross-country link from Alton to Winchester, which had connections to London. It was a single-line service, with loops at stations. Things stayed virtually unchanged until the 1930s. When electrification reached Alton, in 1937, it did not spread down the Watercress Line. Much of the running that followed was a push-pull service, with the engine at one end of a two-carriage train.

During both world wars, because of its

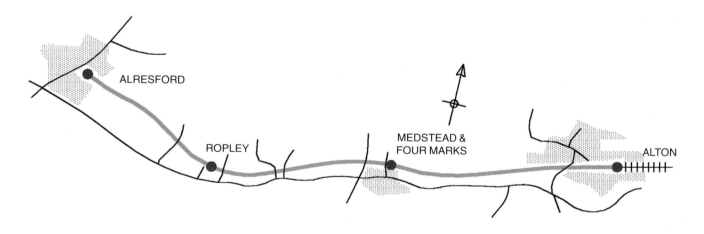

proximity to Aldershot and the south coast, the line was much used for war traffic. In the build-up to D-Day in 1944, it saw a constant stream of trains laden with tanks and equipment.

After the war, there were about seven passenger trains a day, in each direction. This sort of service continued until 1957, when British Railways introduced diesel trains, in order to improve commuter connections to Alton, and hourly trains ran. This service helped the line to survive the Beeching Report closures of 1963. The competition with road traffic was too much, however, and the end was inevitable. The last train ran on 4 February 1973.

Local enthusiasts had been considering preservation for a while, and organizations were set up in order to attempt this. By 1975, share issues were set up, and the second of these was successful. There was enough money to purchase track and trackbed, with deposits placed on further land and buildings. The railway was now operated by the Mid-Hants Railway Preservation Society, who co-ordinate the services of volunteers.

To get the railway operational, and restore the line, buildings and signalling to shape, a

A veteran of war service, and use by the Polish and Greek railways. No. 3278 has been with the Mid-Hants Railway since 1984.

View of S160 No. 3278 'Franklin D. Roosevelt' at Alresford from the footbridge.

mammoth effort was needed. The challenge was met by volunteers in 1976, a Light Railway Order was obtained in early 1977, and the grand opening followed on 30 April 1977.

From the early days, it had been the railway's ambition to extend the service back to Alton, to link with BR's trackwork and passenger connections. All efforts were made to do this.

After the purchase of the line, the next problem was to obtain engines and rolling stock, as well as an engine shed and workshops. After a couple of years' operation, and some energetic fund-raising, an engine shed was built at Ropley. Further engines were obtained from the scrap yard at Barry, in South Wales.

The extension of the railway to Alton got underway in 1982, again, requiring a huge effort from the volunteers. In May 1982, track laying started from Ropley to Medstead and Four Marks Station, about 3 miles (5km), with completion by 1983. On 28 May 1983, the first train ran into Medstead and Four Marks, to the delight of the volunteers who had laid the track. The laying of a further 4½

The USA War Service 'S160s'

British locomotive builders could not meet the demand for war-time engines. With the likelihood of an Allied invasion of the Continent, large numbers were required for home and overseas use. Three big American locomotive works stepped in to meet the demand. The Alco, Baldwin and Lima companies had suffered the effects of the 1930s slump, and were glad to take the orders. A production schedule was very quickly established. The first orders were placed in 1942, and the US Army Transportation Corps (USATC) took control of development. The 2-8-0 engine was small compared with the giants that were made for the US home market.

During the war, more than 2,000 examples were built and distributed all over the northern hemisphere. Between 1942 and 1944, large numbers were used in Britain, although teething troubles and non-compatibility with the British system made them unpopular with the crews, and many modifications had to be incorporated. Three incidents of boiler explosions did not help.

By 1944, they were being diverted abroad with the invading forces. Only one remained in Britain, with the Longmoor Military Railway, but was later scrapped.

Ex-USATC 3278 'Franklin D. Roosevelt' is now in service with the Mid-Hants Railway. This locomotive was recovered from a Greek scrapyard in 1984, after seeing war service in Italy, and then being sold to the Polish railway. There are four other examples of the type preserved in Britain, all recovered from eastern Europe, at the North York Moors Railway, the Worth Valley Railway, the East Lancs Railway and the Llangollen Railway.

miles (7km) of track to Alton started in March 1984, and was completed on the 12 April 1985.

The Mid-Hants Railway was complete, and the completed line was opened officially on 24 July 1985.

Ropley Station is the work centre of the Mid-Hants Railway, where the locomotives and rolling stock are stored and repaired. The high embankment on the north side of the line gives an excellent overall view of proceedings, while visitors are encouraged to look around the works area. Many passengers break their journey to do this.

The art form of topiary is well in evidence on the platform. This, a feature of the railway in pre-preservation days, was reinstated by the Mid-Hants Railway. The signal standards at Ropley are the authentic Southern Railway lattice-post type, with lower as well as higher downward quadrant signal arms.

Unrebuilt West Country Pacific No. 34105 'Swanage' at Ropley, heading a service to Alton. For the VE50 commemoration period at the Mid-Hants Railway, this engine took the identity of its sister engine, Battle of Britain No. 34051 'Sir Winston Churchill', borrowing its name and numberplates.

Pulling into Ropley Station with a rake of Mark 2 coaches is BR Standard 5 No. 73096, temporarily borrowing the identity of No. 73080 'Merlin'.

SR N-Class Maunsell Mogul No. 31874 prepares for the role of 'James the Red Engine'.

Visiting engine GWR Castle Class No. 5080 'Defiant', climbing the one in eighty gradient up to Ropley.

No. 41312 2-6-2T, built at Crewe in 1952, taking a scheduled service as duty engine of the day on 24 July 1999. The front styling is Ivatt, this being the tank version of the Ivatt Mogul.

S160 No. 3278 'Franklin D. Roosevelt' approaching a train at Alresford.

A typical stove-enamelled sign from the past.

A poster at one of the wartime events.

Topiary was a feature at Ropley Station in the past and has been retained by the preservation society.

Left: 'Thomas' and 'James' stand in readiness outside the Ropley shed, seen from the picnic area.

Right: Modified Austerity tank engine, now masquerading as 'Thomas', keeping a careful eye on proceedings during its check-over at Ropley sheds.

CHAPTER EIGHT

Swanage Railway

One of the best sights on Britain's south coast, with a never-ending stream of visitors, is the Dorset gem of Corfe Castle. Originating from the time of William the Conqueror, it can now be reached by steam train on the Swanage Railway.

For many years, the Swanage Railway maintained a low profile, running between Swanage and Harmans Cross, in the middle of nowhere. It has finally broken out of years of financial strife, and all the difficulties that go with it. It now has an extension open, running past the castle to the newly created station of Norden, and its future looks bright. The long-term ambition is to take the line on to Wareham, and connect it with the national network.

The village of Corfe is so small that there are virtually no car-parking facilities, and that includes the station. This problem proved to be a stumbling block in the railway's attempt to reopen Corfe Station. The answer was to build the new station of Norden, a mile past Corfe, with ample car parking, and this has, in effect, provided a 'park and ride' scheme. This has proved to be very successful, as visitors to the castle and Swanage visitors can both join the trains here.

Swanage Station is right in the heart of the town, and parking there is also a problem. The original Swanage Station dates from the opening of the railway in 1885, but was largely rebuilt in 1937, in order to cope with demand. Closure by BR came in 1972, after the station had featured in Dr Beeching's infamous report a decade earlier. The locals, however, wanted a railway for their town. By 1975, a group of determined individuals had formed the Swanage Railway Society, and had secured a licence to reopen Swanage Station site.

For a long while, the fact that the locomotives and rolling stock had to be serviced and prepared right by the station in the town centre caused planning problems.

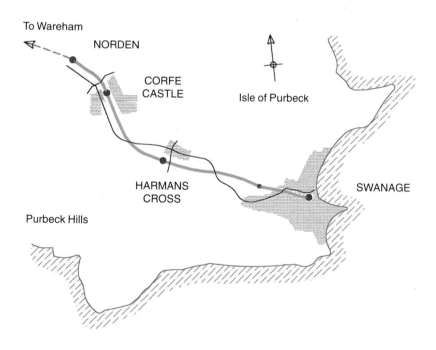

To Wareham

NORDEN

CORFE
CASTLE

Isle of Purbeck

HARMANS
CROSS

SWANAGE

Purbeck Hills

The Bulleid Pacifics

The Bulleid Pacifics were the only Pacifics to be built by the Southern Railway. There were three types: the heavy Merchant Navy Class, and the lighter Battle of Britain and West Country variations, all built with air-smoothed casing.

The Pacific, a revolutionary design, especially in war-time, was introduced in 1941 by O.V. Bulleid for the West Country passenger express trains from London's Waterloo. It caught the imagination of the public and railway staff alike. Among its innovations were electric lighting, chain-driven valve gear and cast wheels.

The torturous gradients west of Salisbury demanded the power of a 'Merchant Navy', while the 'Lights' would take the split trains on from Exeter. These were also suitable for the shorter express train duties from London to the south coast.

Of all of the 140 examples of these classes that were built, an incredible thirty-one survive today, largely thanks to Dai Woodham at the Barry scrapyard. He was sitting on twenty-eight of them.

In the late 1950s, most of these locomotives were rebuilt. In most cases, the streamlined casing was removed, as it had proved to be a problem in servicing the engines. A total of ninety of the classes had the casing permanently removed. Of those now preserved, ten are of the un-rebuilt variety (*see* Great Central Railway, pages [90-95], for examples of the rebuilt engines).

Dugaid Drummond No. 30053 pulls a train into Corfe Castle Station.

Passing the former goods-yard site, which now has a supermarket built on it, Light Pacific No. 34072 '257 Squadron' approaches Swanage Station with a cab-full of trainee drivers. Losing the land to commerce was a small price for the railway's successful preservation.

Eventually, everything was solved, with the siting of the workshops and preparation areas just past the Northbrook Road bridge. Part of the station area could then be sold off to a supermarket company for building.

During the war, the railway had many

The Dugaid Drummond M7 Class

No. 30053, built in 1905, first appeared on the branch line in 1964, before being shipped to Steamtown, Pennsylvania, in 1967. Two decades later, it was purchased by the Swanage Railway and returned to service on the Swanage line in 1987. Now one of the mainstays of the line, 30053 has been in regular service, partnering '257 Squadron'.

important visitors, including General Patton of the US Army, who emerged from the station wearing his pearl-handled revolvers. This was during the build up to D-Day, when the US First Infantry was billeted in the town.

Pride of place among the railway's motive power goes to the superb Battle of Britain Class Pacific engine No. 34072, '257 Squadron'. There could not be a better or more representative locomotive, in its authentic Southern Region setting.

When completed, the Swanage Railway will be the classic branch line, linking the main line to a seaside resort. Holidaymakers and visitors will once again be able to travel by train, and perhaps one day there may be steam excursions from London Waterloo.

The nameplate from the side of No. 34072.

This image of Corfe Castle comes into view shortly after the train has left Norden Station. The line that passes Corfe Castle was re-opened in 1995.

This former Station Master's house at Swanage Station is now part of the office, booking hall, restaurant and shop complex.

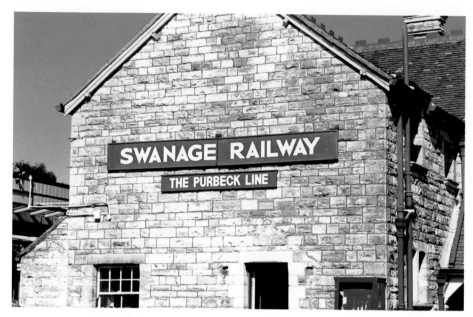

The SR parcels van now stands in the bay platform at Swanage Station and is used for exhibition purposes.

In the low evening light 'M7' No. 30053 hurries past the engine shed with the last train of the day. Battle of Britain No. 43072 '257 Squadron' is on the turntable.

Bulleid Light Pacific '257 Squadron' stands at the buffers at Swanage Station on completion of the run from Norden.

CHAPTER NINE

North York Moors Railway

Grosmont (pronounced 'Growmont') is the headquarters of the North York Moors Railway, and the northern terminus. Visitors can walk through the original George Stephenson tunnel, built for horse-drawn trains, to see the engine sheds and workshops. Opened in 1836, the tunnel soon became obsolete, and a new one was planned for steam trains. This new structure

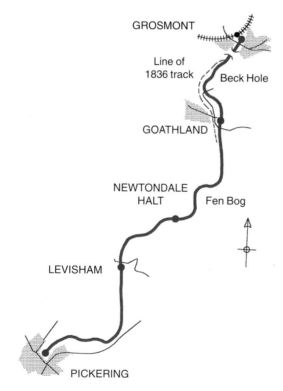

GROSMONT

Line of
1836 track   Beck Hole

GOATHLAND

NEWTONDALE
HALT   Fen Bog

LEVISHAM

PICKERING

was built with the coming of steam in 1845, and was so overpowering that for a long time the village was known simply as 'Tunnel'.

At this time, the trackbed was also re-routed between Grosmont and Goathland. The old trackbed, which had become unworkable, is now a very popular walking trail, passing through an area steeped in industrial history. The old line had to overcome a section of track at an incline of one in ten on the approach to Goathland. Obviously, horses could not pull the carriages up this, so a counterbalanced, water-filled tank on wheels was incorporated. Via a rope around a giant pulley, the weight of the tank going down the slope would pull the carriages up. Later, the carriages were pulled by a steam engine but, after several nasty accidents caused by the rope breaking, and runaway carriages, it was decided to build a new line.

The 'deviation' line was completed in 1865 with the opening of Goathland Station. Construction of the new section was not without its severe problems. To make a workable steam railway, a route had to be blasted through rock. Because of the way the ground rose up to Goathland, the railway still had to contend with a gradient of one in forty-nine.

With the long heavy trains that are needed to run the railway today, this still presents drivers with enormous problems. The passengers, though, are enthralled by the sound of the engines having to put in so much effort.

From Goathland, the deviation line follows practically the same route as the original, for which Stephenson had had to overcome the

hazards of hill, water and the notorious Fen Bog. The volunteer track-laying gangs who rebuilt the line in the 1970s can be proud to be linked with Stephenson's navvies, re-creating railway history. Such gangs developed a wonderful camaraderie; clearing trackbed and laying tracks over such a distance is a task that requires great dedication.

It was about 1967 when thoughts first turned to preservation. A small group of people decided that the line was too important to die, passing through such spectacular scenery, and being steeped in so much history. Fund-raising schemes were set up, people with influence were recruited, together with an ever-growing band of enthusiasts, and the project got under way. It turned out to be one of the great preservation achievements, and in 1973 the NYMR was opened by the Duchess of Kent.

Pickering is the terminus at the southern end of the line, although it had been a

SR 4-4-0 Schools Class

Introduced in 1930, these engines were originally designed to cope with the severe width restrictions of the London to Hastings line. Minimal width and raked sides to the driver's cab assisted to give the clearance needed to pass the very narrow Mountfield and Bo-Peep Tunnels near Hastings. The trains even had special narrow carriages.

With three cylinders, they proved to be strong pullers, and were soon seen working on all the southern routes out of London to the coast.

A total of forty of this prestigious class were built, all being named after public schools. As No. 926, 'Repton' was out-shopped from Eastleigh Works in 1934, to serve right through to withdrawal in 1962. Its first twenty-three years into preservation were spent in Bellows Falls, USA, before it was re-sold and returned to Britain in 1989, where it became resident at the North Yorkshire Railway.

Schools class No. 30926 'Repton' running around the train at Pickering.

Drought conditions will put restrictions on steam running across the moors owing to fire risks. Here in August 1995, WD 2-10-0 No. 90775 gives way to the BR Class 25 D7541 'The Diana' for the Goathland to Levisham section of the line.

'through' station in BR days, when it was part of the Whitby to York line. It once had an overall roof, but this was removed in 1952, and replaced with canopies over the platforms. A trust has now been set up to rebuild the roof in a style closer to its former design. The stone side walls are still in place, although some erosion has taken place, since it has been exposed to the elements for so long.

Goathland has now found new fame as the setting for the television series *Heartbeat*, originally starring Nick Berry. The railway has often been featured in the programme, and is therefore attracting even more visitors to the area.

Long stretches of the line, which snakes through the heart of the moors between Goathland and Levisham, are virtually inaccessible to road and foot travellers. Many hikers use the railway for the first part of a trip. Guides are published highlighting the walks available from the stations along the line, to places of outstanding interest and beauty.

There is still opportunity for expansion at the railway. The line was originally double-tracked, and much thought is now going into re-creating double-tracking, at least for some parts of the line. With the numbers of people being attracted to the railway always increasing, the challenge for the future is how to accommodate extra passengers.

The WD Austerity 2-10-0

Although the 2-8-0 8Fs were successful engines, their axle loading put limitations on their use. Another locomotive was required, and the task of development was given to R.A. Riddles.

The Ministry of Supply wanted a powerful heavy freight engine, for use at home and abroad. It needed to be able to work over lightly laid track, or lines with weak bridges, and should therefore have an axle loading of not more than thirteen tons.

Riddles' answer was a 2-10-0 locomotive, of which 150 were built, all at the Hyde Park Works, Glasgow. Most did service in Britain before being taken abroad to help with the Allied liberation of Europe.

The only drawback with a set of ten coupled driving wheels was the radius of curve that the engine could take. To help overcome this restriction, the centre wheels were flangeless, and the second and fourth driving wheels were shallow-flanged. Other innovations were incorporated, such as a wide firebox and rocking grate, for easy removal of fire remains.

The North Yorkshire Moors Railway has been running two examples of this class, both of which came back to Britain from Greece in 1984: No. 90775 was formerly WD 601, named 'Sturdee', while WD 3672 'Dame Vera Lynn' saw war service in Egypt.

Some spartan fittings were used in the manufacture of these engines, such as a tiny chimney and cast front wheels. These really did give them the 'austerity' appearance. They were designed for speed of manufacture, and prefabricated parts were used wherever possible.

One other notable example in preservation is No. 600 'Gordon'. This is now with the Severn Valley Railway and was originally a training locomotive on the Longmoor Military Railway. R.A. Riddles was later to become the Chief Mechanical Engineer of the newly formed British Railways in 1948. He was instrumental in producing the British Standard types, and one of those was the 9F 2-10-0 Class. It was obvious from the many similarities that the 9F design was based on the war-time version.

Black Five No. 5428 'Eric Treacy', named after the famous railway photographer who was also the Bishop of Wakefield. In their days before preservation very few of the Black Fives were given names. Here seen at Grosmont getting prepared for the Saturday evening running of 'The North Yorkshireman', a very popular steam-hauled dining service.

Front view of Schools Class No. 30926 'Repton'.

Engines made for war. The simple cast wheels and tiny chimney add to the austere appearance of WD 3672.

The pulling power of 2-10-0 Austerity locomotive No. 90775 makes it an ideal engine for the severe North York Moors Railway gradients.

A visitor from the Great Central, Bulleid Pacific No. 34101 'Hartland', one of the West Country Class built for the longer-distance routes on the Southern Railway. Lighter than their sister engines, the 'Merchant Navy' class, they could be used on all express routes on the railway. Many of them, including 34101, were rebuilt and modified in the late 1950s, when their flat panel casings were removed.

Rebuilt Bulleid Pacific No. 34101 'Hartland' at the coaling-stage at Grosmont sheds.

A luggage trolley from the original railway is on the platform at Goathland Station.

A poster advertising the great east coast express train, the 'Flying Scotsman'.

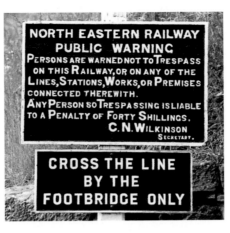

What all the fuss is about! The lineside board indicates that the Goathland Station track slopes at 1 in 138, and then gives way to the severe 1 in 49 gradient.

Warning signs for passengers, at Goathland Station.

An example of wrought iron fish-bellied rail is displayed at Pickering station. It is as the original George Stephenson rail for the horse-drawn wagon-ways.

LNER T3 0-8-0 No. 901, about to enter the big tunnel at Grosmont. No. 901 was built at Darlington in 1919 to serve the heavy workings of the South Yorkshire coal pits. The engine was BR No. 63460 in later years, and was withdrawn from service in 1962, having been working iron-ore trains at Consett. Now part of the National Collection, No. 901 was restored by the NELPG at Grosmont.

The stark austerity lines of the W. D. 2-10-0 'Dame Vera Lynn'.

Bulleid Pacific No. 34101 'Hartland' has been brought to a dead stop at the top of the one in forty-nine gradient, and is having great difficulty getting moving again. WD 90775 patiently waits in the other platform, and the onlookers gaze in amazement at all the effort being put in without much movement (note the Catch Points).

The entrance to the original 1836 George Stephenson tunnel built for horse-drawn trains, now the public walkway to the shed area of the railway.

Grosmont Station from the top of the big tunnel. WD loco 90775 stands in the station waiting to depart with the next train to Pickering. In the foreground is the bridge over the Murk Esk river. To the right is the footpath which follows the trail of the George Stephenson horse-drawn line. There is also the entrance to the original tunnel built in 1836.

The S160 2-8-0 ex-USATC No. 3278 heads a train out of Grosmont and getting up speed for the climb to Goathland.

CHAPTER TEN

East Lancs Railway

A late starter among preserved railways, the East Lancs Railway is now one of the fastest-rising. Aided by the keenness of three local authorities, all the preservationists' dreams are being realized. Once Bury and Rossendale Councils saw the potential of having a steam railway in their area, their cooperation with the preservationists was unstinting. Grants and planning

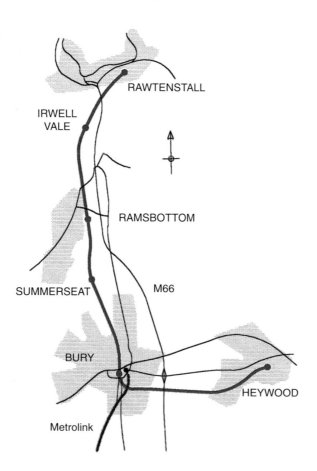

permission have been forthcoming, and the councils have also used the opportunity to upgrade many run-down areas close to the railway.

The towns along the Irwell Valley, which were once at the heart of Lancashire's textile and paper-making industries, suffered severe depression after the decline of those industries. The re-birth of the railway has produced an economic miracle. Revitalization has taken place for small businesses, shops, industry, which includes tourism. Twenty years ago, it would have been difficult to predict that the Irwell Valley would become a tourist boom area.

Bury Council backed the preservationists from the start, while Rochdale Council quickly encouraged the ELR with its planned extension to Heywood, which is scheduled to open in the year 2000. The trackwork has been in place for some time, with a connection to the Railtrack network. This has been used for some time for stock movements, and opens new opportunities for the railway for mainline excursions. Also there is the possibility of running the ELR beyond Heywood, and down the main line to Rochdale Station. Perhaps in the future the ELR might be involved in commuter work, or park and ride schemes.

The railway has also obtained a large engineering workshop at Buckley Wells. The building is a genuine loco works, unique to preservation railways, and Bury Council has helped the ELR to get it. BR had recognized the financial potential in flattening the site,

and selling it on at a premium price, but Bury Council put a Class 2 Preservation Order on it. This reduced the value, and the ELR was able to afford to buy it.

Because of the connection to the main line, and its extensive storage and workshop facilities, this railway is a popular home base for the owners of some of the finest large locomotives. The fact that they often run on the line brings great benefits, and the ELR big engine galas have become almost legendary.

The ELR was a late starter among preserved lines (it did not open until 1987, after eighteen years of struggle), and it therefore found that diesel locomotives were easier to obtain. At first, these were more prominent on the line, with a collection including examples of most of the types that were in use in the 1950s and 1960s. The Bolton St Station

The 5MT Class 2-6-0

These 'Crabs' were so nicknamed because the cylinders and valve gear were placed at an angle high on the sides of the engines. This class was the first to be developed by the LMS after Grouping in 1923. Between 1926 and 1932, 245 were built at Crewe and Horwich, and they lasted in large numbers right through to the 1960s.

The Midland Region trainspotters were among the most dedicated of all. They needed to be, because their region had the widest spread of the four, reaching from Scotland right down to London and Bath in the south. The 'Crabs' were spread far and wide, and they took some finding.

Right up until the end of steam the Midland lads were out on 'Crab' hunts, trying to complete their set. A 'Crab' chase these days is less demanding, as there are now only three left.

Ivatt No. 46441 arrives at Ramsbottom with the southbound service, while No. 42765 waits for clearance with the train north.

'Crab' No. 42765 standing at Ramsbottom.

reflects this period in its architecture. The railway is happy to operate both diesels and steam, which is authentic for the period. There is a very keen enthusiast following for diesels, and these also have their gala days and weekends.

In 1972, the last passenger train ran between Bury and Rawtenstall before closure. The East Lancs Preservation Society had been formed in 1968, to set up a railway museum at Castle Croft goods yard, and with the distant hope of saving the line. It took well into the 1980s before things started to happen, but the close partnership with the local councils has led to exciting developments.

New stations were built to the highest standards, in a style sympathetic to the ELR of old. There was no compromise on quality, and the awards that have been bestowed on the project prove this.

The new extension to Heywood has given the railway a 12-mile (19-km) running length, and it can accommodate a nine-carriage train. The extension makes for a very interesting journey. After leaving Bolton St Station, the line turns left. It then has to cross the paths of the Manchester Road, and the Metrolink Railway, which are on about the same level as the ELR. This was achieved by ramping down, to get under the Manchester Road, climbing up at an astonishing one in twenty-five, to bridge over the Metrolink, and descending down the other side at a incline of one in thirty-five. The line then crosses the M66 by the seven-arch Roch Viaduct.

These inclines are among the severest on any standard-gauge preserved line in Britain, making a very interesting ride. The strongest of engines will be needed, and a banking engine ought not to be far away.

The Ivatt Mogul

H.G. Ivatt was the last Superintendent of the London, Midland and Scottish Railway. He brought out two versions of this Class 2 locomotive, a 2-6-0 and a 2-6-2 tank. (All 2-6-0 engines are called Moguls.) They continued to be built after nationalization right through to 1953. So successful were these engines for cross-country and short-haul routes, that the designs were adopted as BR Standard types. The new ones became the 78000 and 84000 Classes.

There was also a heavier Ivatt Class 4 type, the design of which (with modifications) was to become the BS 76000 Class. An example of the Ivatt 2-6-2 tank can now be seen in action at the Mid-Hants Railway.

Ivatt Mogul No. 46441 backs on to a train at Bury for the run to Rawtenstall.

The superbly turned out maroon Ivatt Mogul No. 46441, standing at Ramsbottom.

October gala day at the ELR – Black Five 5407 and 71000 'Duke of Gloucester' dash through to Bolton Street.

D1074 'Western Statesman' and Hymek D7076 stand by the diesel shed at Bury.

The clearest of information is given from this old train indicator at Bury Station.

Ivatt Mogul No. 46441 arriving at Rawtenstall. When the ELR set out on its rebuilding programme, the aim was to recapture the ELR of old. The new clocktower is in the style of the former LYR clock at Bury.

'Crab' No. 42765 stands at the north end of Platform 2 at Bolton St Station, one of the most atmospheric locations on the preserved railways, giving a true period feel of the 1950s and 1960s.

Ramsbottom Station seeks and attains the highest standards, and has won many awards.

CHAPTER ELEVEN

Severn Valley Railway

The Severn Valley Railway is the classic steam railway, with all the engines and rolling stock and, not least, a 16-mile (26km) scenic route that passes through some of Britain's most picturesque countryside. Some 200 volunteers, together with a contingent of permanent staff, run the railway with skill and great efficiency.

The line begins at the new station of Kidderminster, situated across the forecourt from the mainline station. The new building was built in 1984 to an Edwardian design, on the site of a former goods yard. It is a terminus that every other railway would like to have. As well as the outer forecourt, there is an inner concourse, the King and Castle pub, a refreshment room, a bookstall and a relic shop. Also on the site is a miniature railway and a Great Western museum. The area is perfect for feature displays, and these are often organized.

At the other end of the line is the original SVR station of Bridgnorth, which the society took over in 1965. On the north side is the engine shed, and the preparation area. From the footbridge, early visitors will see the engines being fired up. The comings and goings from the shed make fascinating viewing all day. Engine preparation is something an ordinary traveller would never have seen in the days of steam. At an enthusiasts' event at the SVR, there may be up to ten engines in steam on one day.

Also at Bridgnorth Station is another pub owned by the railway, the Railwayman's Arms, which survives from the days of British Railways.

The original railway ran for 101 years, until it was closed to passengers in 1963, a victim of the Dr Beeching report. At the end, it was hardly being used at all, and was never financially successful. Typical workings would be four trains a day in each direction. Absorbed into the GWR in the 1870s, it was linked to Kidderminster in 1878. The line also

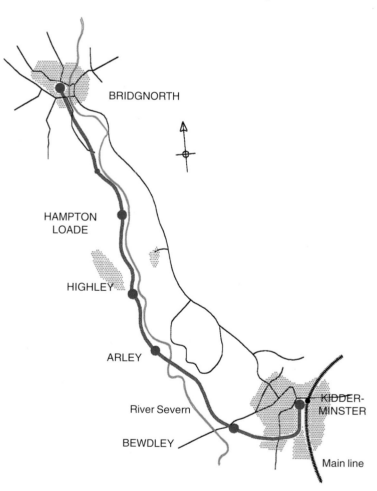

BRIDGNORTH

HAMPTON
LOADE

HIGHLEY

ARLEY

River Severn

BEWDLEY

KIDDER-
MINSTER

Main line

served freight and coal, with Alveley Colliery using it until the pit closure in 1969.

By the mid- to late 1960s, the preservationists were well under way with saving the line. The Severn Valley Preservation Society was set up by a group of enthusiasts in Kidderminster in 1965. With many money-making schemes well advanced, the first stock was bought in 1967. It took three more years to upgrade the railway to operating condition and obtain a Light Railway Order. Legislation was difficult, as the authorities had to be sure that all safety conditions were met, but by 1970 the preserved railway was up and running.

With the initial section open between Bridgnorth and Hampton Loade, all efforts were being made to extend onwards. The fact that the line through to Bewdley was open in 1974 represents a terrific achievement by the

GWR 73XX Class No. 7325 arriving at Arley with a train from Bridgnorth. Alongside is the ex-LNER teak-bodied coach stock.

A working signal box frame exhibited in the Great Western Museum at Kidderminster Station.

These ladies are enjoying a break during the activities at Kidderminster Station.

volunteers. The railway by that time had grown to over 12 miles (19km) long.

The line to Foley Park, with its connection to the main network, had been purchased in 1974. For the next few years, this was used only for special excursions and stock deliveries. Bewdley had the facilities for use as a turnaround point, and became the terminus for traffic, also in 1974.

Ten years later, Kidderminster was reached. A share issue was set up in 1983, and proved to be very successful. It not only enabled the purchase of an extra section of line to Kidderminster, but also financed the building of a superb terminus building. The railway was complete.

At one time, the plan had been to extend northwards towards Ironbridge. This has, however, proved to be impossible, with too many new roads and houses blocking the way.

The latest expansion of the railway is the construction of a magnificent carriage shed at Kidderminster. With the aid of a £1.75m heritage lottery grant, the large fleet of historic carriages can now be kept and restored under cover.

Railway coaches have been somewhat overlooked in the growth of most preserved lines – stations, track and motive power are seen as the first essentials. The SVR has now addressed this. Many of these craftsman-built vehicles are of timber construction, with fabric roofs. Many new rail volunteers will find their niche in acquiring the old skills of coach-building.

Every locomotive is required to have a current ten-year boiler certificate before it can be put to work on a train. Before awarding the certificate, the Railway Inspectorate insists on lifting the boiler from its frame and inspecting it to its satisfaction. At Bridgnorth, the SVR has one of the leading engineering depots of its kind. At the time of a boiler inspection, an engine will also be given a full inspection. The SVR engine shop is capable of all the major tasks. As well as boilersmith skills, such tasks as wheel turning, cylinder boring and refurbishment of motion parts are undertaken. The works are so efficient that locos from other railways are regularly taken in on a contract basis.

This is probably the finest preserved railway in the country, in terms of efficiency, scenery, buildings and authenticity. It is easy now just to think of it as a commercial business. But never should be forgotten all those volunteers who gave it the big push in the early 1970s, or the fact that all the operating side of the railway is run by volunteers.

Kidderminster Station

The SVR showed the way for preserved railways, with the building of its new terminus to a period design. Built right in the town centre opposite the mainline station, it is the perfect attraction for tourists. The internal courtyard is an ideal setting for functions. Site facilities include the King and Castle pub, and a museum crammed full of anything that bears the 'Great Western Railway' name, crest or initials.

Forecourt activity straight from the 1940s.

Various forms of transport are parked outside Kidderminster Station, including the military.

At one time one of these would be in every goods yard in the country. The Scammell Mechanical Horse.

Two ladies seemingly not too impressed with the wartime news.

The Scammell 'Mechanical Horse'

Developed in the 1930s to replace the horse, this vehicle soon became a fixture in nearly every goods yard in Britain. Its great advantages were that it could turn in a very small space, and that trailers were easily detached from it. Its disadvantages, for a motor vehicle, were that it did not have a self-starter, and was also quite slow.

The picturesque country branch-line
station at Arley.

The British Railways lion and wheel logo, adopted on all
regions after nationalization in 1948.

A4 Class 'Union of South Africa' is currently the only surviving
member of its class to be painted in BR green. A regular performer
on steam specials, No. 60009 is at present based at the SVR.

No. 80079 2-6-4T being prepared at the Bridgnorth shed. A4 Class Pacific 'Union of South Africa' is in the background.

GWR 'Manor' Class No. 7802 'Bradley Manor' crossing the famous Victoria Bridge with a southbound train.

British Standard Class '4' 2-6-4T

No. 80079 was one of 155 of this class, which was based on the Fowler-Stanier-Fairburn locos of similar design. The locomotive soon proved to be very popular, and examples were spread over the country, with the exception of the Western Region. Built at Brighton in 1954, 80079 spent much of its life on the London, Tilbury and Southend line.

In more recent times it has taken part in the parallel running event 'Steam on the Met', as well as taking part in other mainline rail tours. It was purchased for the SVR in 1970 from the Woodham Bros scrapyard in South Wales and entered service in 1977, after restoration.

CHAPTER TWELVE

South Devon Railway

Before 1991 this line was, appropriately, called the Dart Valley Railway. The track follows the picturesque River Dart for all its 7-mile (11km) length between Buckfastleigh and Totnes. Formerly a 9½-mile (15km) branch line, built in 1872 as part of Brunel's broad-gauge system, it served the woollen mills along the river, right up to Ashburton. The end section up to Ashburton

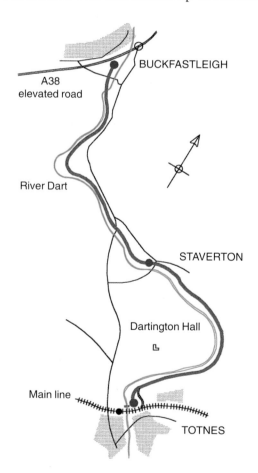

has now been swallowed up under the A38 trunk road scheme.

After its closure to passengers by BR in 1958 (1962 for freight traffic), a group of fourteen businessmen got together with the aim of reopening the line as a commercial venture. Events overtook this first group, and by 1966 the aim was to get the line reopened, to be run by volunteers. The Dart Valley Railway Association became the organizing body. Rolling stock had been obtained, and locomotives 4555 and 3205 were on their way. All hands were needed to clear the track, upgrade the stations, and prepare working areas. A Light Railway Order was needed, and obtained through British Railways. On 5 April 1969 the Dart Valley Light Railway Ltd was opened by Dr Beeching.

The line was in operation, but it did not have a suitable terminus station with run-around loops at both ends. It started with a typical GWR push-pull auto-train service, with tank engine attached. This could only accommodate two coaches, as there had to be rod connections to the cab at the end of the train. Sometimes the train would run with two coaches on both sides of the engine. This was unpopular, and all efforts were made to provide proper facilities, with runaround loops, at each end of the line. This was achieved in 1970, and a normal style of service was provided.

The DVLR was able to acquire the Paignton to Kingswear branch from BR in 1972, and the company found itself in control of two railways. Over the next few years the

Paignton line was to gain in prestige, while the Dart Valley Railway was fighting for profitability.

In 1985, BR allowed the DVR to share Totnes Station. At the time, this seemed to be the answer to all their problems, but the charges involved led the railway into a loss-making situation, and to the brink of closure. The use of Totnes Station was abandoned.

With the Paignton line still gaining, the Dart Valley Light Railway decided by 1990 to concentrate on the Paignton line, and offer the DVR to a new operator. The volunteers were able to become the operators through the company Dumbleton Hall Locomotive Ltd. This was a company with charitable status, which was allowed to run a railway. On 1 January 1991, it became the South Devon Railway Trust, and the railway was renamed South Devon Railway.

Since then, the railway has moved forward. Now eligible for grants, and with energetic fund raising, much progress has been made. Included in the developments is a much-needed footbridge across the river at Totnes, which links the new terminus to the town.

Buckfastleigh Station is thriving. The station has been restored in traditional style, and includes an impressive museum, full of Great Western relics. Among its exhibits is the only surviving locomotive from the broad-gauge days – a vertical-boilered engine called 'Tiny'.

Visitors to the Buckfastleigh complex can look around the engine sheds, which house a fascinating selection of locos and rolling stock, and view the workshops, to admire the skills and efforts of the volunteers. Also within the Buckfastleigh complex are picnic areas, a maze and a children's play area.

WD132 'Sapper', formerly of the Bicester Military Railway, one of the two ex-WD Hunslet Austerity saddle tanks operational at the SDR. The other is BR No. 68011 'Errol Lonsdale', the engine that found fame by appearing in the film *The Great St Trinians Train Robbery*.

The Hunslet Austerity
locomotive 'Sapper' at
Buckfastleigh.

Since October 1995, the railway was again able to run an auto-train, and re-enact scenes from the birth of the DVR. No other railway provides this spectacle over a former branch line.

With the addition of a runaround loop at Staverton, dual train workings are now available, which opens up the scope of operations. It is now possible to work an intensive timetable.

Axle Loading on the South Devon Railway

For a long time, the SDR was only able to accommodate small locomotives, the loading gauge attributed to the line previously being restricted to 16 tons per axle. The railway has since strengthened many of the bridges on the line, and HM Railway Inspectorate has approved an axle loading of 18 tons per axle.

The decking and stonework re-pointing on the bridge just south of Staverton have long since been completed and approved for 20-ton workings. Now, only the five-arch Nursery Pool bridge needs attention. Once this work is completed and approved, the scope of operations will be dramatically increased, and the whole line should get a 20-ton rating. The railway will then be clear to run its very own No. 4920 'Dumbleton Hall' (18 tons 19 cwt).

The previous increase, to 18 tons per axle, seemed like a breath of fresh air to the railway. It opened doors for the invitation of visiting tender engines; such as the 'Manors' with a loading of 17 tons 5 cwt, and the 4300 Class, at 17 tons 12 cwt. The resident British Standard 2-6-4T No. 80064, at 17 tons 12 cwt, can also be used.

The GWR Auto-Train

The South Devon Railway seeks to retain its authentic image of a Great Western Railway country branch line, and its speciality attraction is the auto-train.

The GWR was to pioneer the running of an engine-less train, and develop the auto-coach. On short branch-line services, the uncoupling of an engine and the 'running around' of a

Dean Forest Prairie tank 5541, waiting at Buckfastleigh watering point, together with Great Western Society Collett 0-4-2 '14XX' No. 1466, on loan from the Didcot Railway Centre.

Replica of the locomotive and train that inaugurated the Stockton and Darlington Railway in 1825, giving rides at Buckfastleigh.

One of the coveted prizes that can be bestowed on a railway, the Ian Allan award, given to Staverton Station.

train for the return trip could be troublesome and time-consuming.

Originally, the auto-coaches were single carriages that ran on their own, under the power of a steam engine within the coach. However, these did not prove to be very successful, as they did not generate enough power. This was especially apparent when a second carriage was attached, or when coping with gradients.

The auto-coaches were soon adapted to be used in conjunction with a tank engine, to be used as a push-pull service. When being pushed, the driver would be in a compartment at the front of the coach, with the fireman in the engine. The driver would control the train with levers and a system of rods passing below the coach, linked to the regulator, and

the vacuum brake. He also had a foot-operated gong, to be used instead of the engine's whistle.

This system had limitations – only a maximum of two coaches could be used at a time, because of difficulties with the rod system. There was a type of universal joint at connections and operation was difficult, especially on bends. The fireman would often have to help the driver out with the workings. If a long train was necessary, it was not unusual for the engine to be in the middle of a four-car unit.

The auto-train system with tank engine was adopted by all the railway regions. It proved to be a very satisfactory method of operation for branch lines, which were essential feeders for the main lines.

Once a common sight in these parts, the auto-train steams towards Staverton on the branch line, which hugs the bank of the River Dart.

One of the most photographed locations along the line, the Nursery Pool bridge. Saddle tank No. 68011 'Errol Lonsdale' takes a scheduled service towards Buckfastleigh.

The SDR's own auto-coach in carmine and cream livery, with driver in the cab, just about to depart from Staverton with the return reverse running service to Buckfastleigh.

Prairie tank and auto-train standing at Buckfastleigh, awaiting the arrival of a return train from Totnes.

Among the exhibits at the Buckfastleigh Museum is the LSWR Beattie No. 0298 2-4-0 well tank, on loan from the National Collection. It is so named because its water tank is situated in the well of the engine's frame. Three of the class, including No. 0298, worked for many years on the Wenford Bridge line in Cornwall serving the china-clay industry.

Great Western tank engine No. 5541 and ex-Longmoor Military Railway, now
numbered BR 68011, wait patiently at Buckfastleigh Station.

The coupling of the auto-train between the
engine and the coach. At the bottom are the
rods the driver in the front of the coach can use
to control the regulator on the engine behind.

The exhibits in the museum include
photographs of how the railway used to be,
and display cases full of GWR silverware.

One exhibit at the Buckfastleigh Museum –
the only surviving former broad-gauge
working locomotive still in existence, the
vertically boilered engine called 'Tiny'.

CHAPTER THIRTEEN

Paignton and Dartmouth Steam Railway

The Paignton and Dartmouth Steam Railway is one railway that everyone wants to visit. It is a typical Great Western branch line, threading its way along the Torbay coast, then passing inland over viaducts, through lush countryside. The line emerges alongside the Dart Estuary, hugging the sea wall, all the way into Kingwear.

This is more than a branch line, however. In

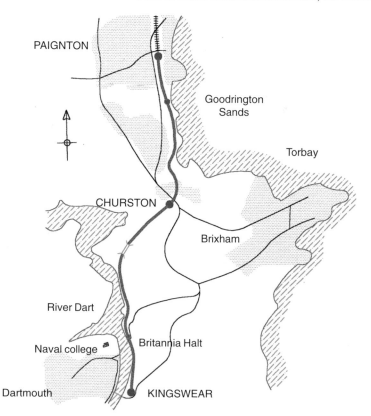

the great days of steam, the classic 'Torbay Express' from Paddington came right along the single line from Paignton, and finished at Kingswear, and the line was therefore built to mainline standards. Even today, it can accommodate the largest engines.

British Railways announced that it was closing the line in 1972. The Dart Valley Railway was able to take it over, virtually without any interruption in service. A new terminus had to be provided at Paignton, and this was squeezed in alongside the mainline station. The line was diverted into the new terminus, and a connection to the main network was left – a prize sought by all preserved railways.

The new station is surprisingly spacious, with a concourse, a large booking hall, a restaurant and a gift shop. It has been kept to a very high standard, and is very inviting to the holidaymakers strolling around the centre of the town.

Devon was served by both the Great Western and Southern Railways, and passengers from London had a choice of services, from either Paddington or Waterloo. Before the days of the affordable European package holiday, Devon and Cornwall were the dream destinations. The big express trains led the way west to the 'English Riviera'. The GWR was generally considered to be the premier service. At peak times, a succession of fourteen coach expresses would leave

Paddington, hauled by either a 'King' or a 'Castle', to deliver holidaymakers. One of these was, of course, the 'Torbay Express'.

The 'Devon Belle' observation coach, which today runs on the Paignton and Dartmouth, used to be featured on the back of a top Southern Railway Pullman train of the same name. This ran from Waterloo to Ilfracombe, via Exeter, where it split, with a section going to Plymouth Friary. The observation coach fitted to the back of the train gave panoramic views of the glorious Devon coastal region.

The preserved line leaves Paignton and moves away from the main line towards Goodrington Sands Halt, passing alongside

GWR Hall Class

The Hall Class was the great general-purpose workhorse of the Great Western Railway. It was the ideal engine for long-distance stopping passenger trains, and also took a turn with freight duties. A powerful two-cylinder loco (with duties similar to those of the LMS 'Black Five'), it was well able to take a fast express train when there was no King or Castle Class available.

A total of 259 of the class were built. At first, they took their names from stately homes all across the GWR region, but they were forced to borrow names from elsewhere when the numbers grew too high!

The superbly turned out No. 4920 'Dumbleton Hall' in the siding beside the entrance at Paignton. The engine re-entered service in 1991, after restoration at the workshops at Buckfastleigh.

5239 'Goliath' taking coal and water before going into service for the day at Paignton.

the water flumes at the leisure park, and the nearby Paignton Zoo. It then climbs along the back of the beach, before turning inland to reach Churston, which is the summit of the line. It is also the passing point when, in peak season, two trains run. Also at Churston is the railway's maintenance depot, the sidings for service stock, and the turntable.

Onwards from Churston, it is downhill all the way to Kingswear. Through the tunnel, and then over the much-photographed Greenway Viaduct, the line drops right down to emerge alongside the River Dart at Britannia Ferry. Here is the small signal cabin that controls the signalling for the whole line. Just across the water is the famous Royal Naval College of Dartmouth. The line then

follows the river edge right into Kingswear.

At one time, Dartmouth itself had a railway station. Built on the opposite side of the river from Kingswear, it was owned by the Great Western Railway, but it was a station without trains. The GWR operated the ferry across to it, until the local council took over this operation. The building is presently being used as a restaurant.

The Dart River has always been a hive of boating activities, and river cruisers connect with the P&DSR. Tickets can be bought at Paignton for joint rail and river round trips.

Kingswear Station is just across the Dart Estuary from Dartmouth and the Britannia Naval College. It was once the end of the line for the famous 'Torbay Express', one of the great named holiday expresses out of London Paddington. Leisure craft share the sheltered waters with naval craft; here, huge numbers of holidaymakers would have arrived by train in times gone by.

The railway was also the lifeline for Dartmouth, just across the river. Provisions, goods, parcels, or even advance luggage for the cadets of the Naval College – the railway brought it all. In the other direction, coal disgorged from boats alongside the jetty was carried.

How could anyone imagine that there was no future for lines like these? Pushed out by the motor vehicle, they are now fighting back. As is the case with so many of the railways that have been saved by preservationists, the P&DSR is now being encouraged to become a public service once more, to help to relieve overcrowded roads. Hopefully, this might mean that one day Kingswear Station will live once again in the public service.

History Note – The Great Expresses to Devon

The 'Cornish Riviera Express', or 'Limited' as the railmen called it, was the pride of the Great Western Railway. Before the east-coast main line went non-stop with the London-Edinburgh run, the London to Plymouth trip of the Cornish Riviera held the distinction of being Britain's longest non-stop scheduled rail journey. Its final destination was Penzance.

In 1926, the King Class of locomotive was introduced, and this increased the train's all-round performance. The train consisted of fourteen carriages, including three slip carriages. These slip carriages would be discharged from the back of the train while it was travelling at speed. One would be slipped at Westbury, another at Taunton and a final one at Exeter. One advantage to the train was that it decreased some of its load just as it was approaching the severe gradients of west Somerset and Devon.

The Cornish Riviera ran right through to the time of the HT125 trains. By then, the time for the 225-mile (360km) run to Plymouth had come down to just over three hours, an hour faster than its steam forerunners.

The 'Cornish Riviera Express' had a regular daily time of 10.30am from Paddington, and the 'Torbay Express' followed in the 12.00pm departure slot. The 'Torbay Express' was invariably pulled by a King, but sometimes a Castle Class was an able deputy for the three-hour non-stop run to Exeter. After Exeter, and stops at Torquay and Paignton, the train turned off on to the single track for the final 6 miles (9.5km) to Kingswear. This stretch is now the preserved line.

It was quite unique for these top Great Western Railway locomotives to take a named express down a stretch of branch line. The 'up' train from Kingswear would depart daily at 11.25am. The local crew would have supervised and checked the preparation of the engine at Newton Abbot, then they would have brought it down to Kingswear, perhaps taking a local train in, before turning and attaching to the main train for the journey.

After taking the train to London, the crew would stay overnight, near the Old Oak Common sheds. On the next day they would pick up the same engine at the shed, and with it take that day's 'Torbay Express' home.

The 'Devon Belle' began in 1947 with an all-Pullman train, aimed at setting the highest standards of service to the West Country. This train was to supplement the long-established 'Atlantic Coast Express' from London Waterloo and add a new dimension to West Country travel. Generally, it was to be pulled by a 'Merchant Navy' engine, to enable it to cope with the steep gradients west of Salisbury.

The first stop was Wilton to change engines, then Sidmouth Junction, and then Exeter Central, where the train split. The lighter West Country Class of engine would then take the trains on to Plymouth and Ilfracombe.

The 'Devon Belle' observation coach was added to the back of the train as a final touch of luxury. It is worth considering the manoeuvre that was necessary to turn the observation coach at the end of each journey, so that the viewing end of the coach was at the back of the train.

The 'Devon Belle' express was relatively short-lived due to a sharp tailing-off of customers. The service was reduced in 1952, and finally ended in 1954.

On the return trip with the engine on the observation end, the train passes Britannia Crossing. The signal cabin of the railway is in the background.

No. 5239 'Goliath' waiting at Paignton. This class were never given names in their original days of service, but 'Goliath' is an appropriate title for an engine with such massive pulling power.

Hugging the sea wall of the Dart Estuary, No. 5239 cruises the final section into Kingswear.

GWR 5205 Class 2-8-0 Tank

No. 5239 'Goliath' was from this class of heavy pulling locomotives, especially designed for the coal fields of South Wales. Developed from the 42xx Churchward Class of 1910, No. 5239 was built at Swindon in 1924, and carried on in service until it was withdrawn by BR in 1963. It then languished at the Barry scrapyard until it was bought by the Dart Valley Railway, in 1973.

It has proved to be ideally suited to the heavy pulling requirements of the long trains and tough gradients of the Paignton line. No. 5239 was reintroduced into service in 1978, when it was given its name. Since then it has been a staunch performer, in a role which is far removed from its days in the dust of the Welsh valleys.

The 'Devon Belle' Observation Car

Originally built in 1917 as an ambulance coach, the 'Devon Belle' observation coach was converted in 1921 into a Pullman car. Later, it was rebuilt again with an observation end, with the intention of using it for the Southern Railway's 'Devon Belle' Pullman train between London Waterloo and Ilfracombe.

This train was finally introduced in 1947 but it was to have a short life. The car was then used on other scenic routes, including some in Wales and Scotland.

'Goliath' entering a cutting through the red sandstone cliffs before turning inland and approaching Churston.

The brightly painted signage at Paignton Station, with the main-line station in the background.

No. 5239 'Goliath' leaving Goodrington Sands Station and beginning the sharp one in seventy climb past the golden sands of Goodrington on the Torbay coast.

Kingswear Station, the end of the line for the Paignton and Dartmouth Railway. The line follows the the sea wall around the harbour. 'Goliath' about to begin the return trip.

CHAPTER FOURTEEN

Great Central Railway

The Great Central Railway is potentially the biggest of all the preserved railways, being the only one to operate over a former premier main line. All efforts and expansion plans have the overall aim of running a re-created double-tracked main line.

From the new station at Leicester North to Loughborough Central Station is a distance of

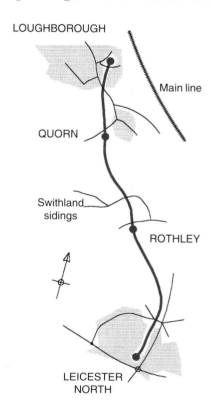

8 miles (13km), and the ambition is to extend further northwards right up to the new Nottingham Heritage Centre at Ruddington, another 9 miles (14.5km). This is for the future, however. The fact that the complexities of the northern extension can be tackled shows how far the preservation movement has come.

At the moment, much thought is being given to replanning and improvements at Leicester North. Previous plans to build a station in a style representative of the former Great Central Railway have had to be shelved. A share issue was set up to finance the plan, but difficulties on the site led to a reduction of the scheme. The new terminus complex will eventually include an engine shed, a visitor centre, a turntable and coaling facilities, as well as shopping and refreshment facilities. Leicester City Council is working very closely with the railway to help develop this site, undoubtedly the major tourist attraction of the area.

Already the railway is able to put on spectacles that are beyond the scope of the opposition. Double tracks are already installed between Loughborough and Quorn, and the aim is to show mainline workings at realistic speeds. Normally, railways operating under the licence of a Light Railway Order are restricted to a speed limit of 25mph (40km/h).

Loughborough Central is a typical station of yesteryear. All the trappings are there, evoking the genuine sights, sounds and smells. Visitors can walk right up to the workshops, and engine sheds, and see the big locomotives being taken in and out of service.

The railway is part of the former mainline route, the original Great Central Railway from Annesley near Nottingham to London Marylebone. Built in the 1890s by Sir Edward Watkin as a southern extension of the Manchester, Sheffield and Lincolnshire Railway, it was a very forward-looking railway, with good stock and a reliable service.

The preserved stretch of line was closed by British Railways in 1969. It was a move that had been inevitable for some time, not only because of the increase in car ownership, but also because the railway was in direct competition with the St Pancras-Nottingham-Sheffield main line.

The British passion for steam was destined again to win through. A group of enthusiasts were prepared to fight to preserve a part of Britain's heritage, with the result that just four years later the line reopened between Loughborough Central and Quorn. Three years after that the section to Rothley opened, with Leicester North being reached in 1991.

Like all the railways, the Great Central has to move with the times, constantly coming up with new ideas to attract customers. One recent introduction is a driver-training course, on which participants can actually drive a big engine. These footplate experiences are proving very popular. There are three different packages, tailored to individual requirements, and dreams really can come true. A trainee can drive a powerful locomotive and eight carriages (or a freight train) from Loughborough to Leicester and back.

The events of the railway, which now go on all year round, are impressively varied,

A double heading of rebuilt Bulleid Pacifics at Leicester North. In the foreground is No.35005SR Merchant Navy Class Canadian Pacific, and behind is West Country Class No. 34039 Boscastle. Note the embryonic linework, which will develop dramatically as time goes on.

Stanier 8F in war-time guise, for the VE Day gala at the Great Central Railway. Former LMS 8F No. 48305 was out-shopped in authentic war-time unlined matt black, carrying the number 7652, its number when it was allocated to run in LNER traffic. War-time re-creations are now a regular and popular annual event at the railway, when many historic engines are turned out in earlier livery.

catering for young and old. Trains can be hired for private functions, or adults can give themselves the treat of an evening meal on a train.

Loughborough Central Station

Loughborough Central Station is one of the great locations of the preservation movement – a place where time seems to have stood still. The only difference between the 1950s and now is that today the locomotives are cherished. All the atmosphere, smell and sounds are here. There are old signals, buildings, steam and soot.

What more could anyone ask?

After a walk down the line, visitors may have the chance to see the engines being prepared. Those big monsters were built in the glory days of the railway, when every big company wanted to do better than the others. In and around the sheds, the volunteers are renovating other engines and stock. It is their skill and dedication that makes all this possible.

At present, Loughborough is the railway's northern terminus, but if the expansion plans are successful, big express trains might one day be seen passing here on a double-track system.

5MT 4-6-0 'Black Five'

The two-cylinder 'Jack of all Trades' of the London Midland and Scottish Railway (later to be the Midland Region), this engine's distinctive whistle left no one in doubt as it approached a station. It was built from 1934 to a taper boiler design, and there were a massive 842 to the class, very few of which had names in BR days. They were spread all across the London Midland Region, and often strayed into other areas.

Less sought after by spotters than the 'Jubilees', the 'Black Fives' were the unsung heroes, always there to take a passenger express if necessary, or to do duty with the constant stream of goods trains that used to be such a big part of the system.

Most of the big centres now have an example in preservation. They are very well represented and, as in their former life, they are always ready to do a turn of duty at a special event, or a steam tour.

Above: **The workhorses of the LMS. The Black 5 class. No. 5231 is looking in fine condition at Loughborough.**

Below: **The 125th Sheffield Guides and Brownies take part in the VE50 celebrations.**

WR Hall Class 'Witherslack Hall' arrives at Leicester North with a passenger service.

The VE50 programme at the Great Central Railway.

The Stanier 8F No. 7652 steams freely out of Loughborough.

Coronation Class Pacific No. 46229 'Duchess of Hamilton', one of only three such engines in preservation, arriving at Leicester North. This class was built by William Stanier from 1937, and was developed from the 'Princess Royal' class. Many, including 46229, received streamlined 'Coronation Scot'-type casings, all of which were removed after the war.

Loughborough Central bookstall with war report placards.

Below: No. 5593 'Kolhapur'. The three-cylinder Jubilee Class was introduced in 1934, for main-line work. Note the special commemorative Silver Jubilee livery of shiny black paintwork with red and chrome trims.

These monster locomotives are of an awesome size. The Bulleid Pacific No. 34039 'Boscastle' outside the Loughborough shed.

Another look at the Stanier 8F in its 'austere' appearance.

A time-warp picture – is it Loughborough Central in the 1990s, or the 1950s? No. 45593 'Kolhapur', painted in BR Standard Brunswick green, about to take a train south on a murky day.

Another day and 'Kolhapur' has a different livery and is numbered 5593. This is for a joint celebration of VE50 and 60th anniversary of the introduction of the Jubilee class of engine.

In war-time livery of unlined matt black, 8F NE No. 7652 trundles across the public footpath to head the next train out of Loughborough Central.

History Note –
The Original Great Central

The original Great Central Railway was founded in 1899 by Edward W. Watkin, who died five years before its opening. Watkin was a visionary whose aim was to extend his northern railway network southwards, with his own line into London, and then on to the Continent via a channel tunnel.

In creating the Great Central Railway, Watkin was competing with some major opposition, in the Midland, the Great Northern and the North Western Railways. In order to compete successfully, and add another terminus to the line of stations above the Royal boundary of Marylebone Road – Euston Road in London (no line was allowed to penetrate this boundary above ground), Watkin had to offer something extra. His solution was to offer a level of style and comfort that had never been seen on the railways, together with a completely new innovation – a buffet annexe added to each carriage.

Following Edward Watkin's death, someone else had to take the lead. Sam Fay became general manager of the GCR in 1902. He brought in the innovations and ran the railway with great efficiency. The trains won a reputation for speed, comfort and punctuality, and Fay was knighted for his services in 1912.

Watkin had earlier secured his railway's future by getting his foot in the door of other railways, with a seat on the board of the Metropolitan and South Eastern Railways, and the chairmanship of the Manchester, Sheffield & Lincolnshire Railway. The MSLR crossed the whole of the north of England, and came south as far as Annesley, near Nottingham. Watkin put a Bill before Parliament to lay a new line from Annesley Road to Quainton Road in Buckinghamshire, conveniently at the far end of his Metropolitan Railway. All that was left was to add in the short stretch at the London end, from Canfield Place to the new terminus. When the new railway opened, on 9 March 1899, the whole of Watkin's northern railway network joined to become part of the Great Central Railway Company.

The coming of the new railway caused much excitement around north London, with speculators gambling on where the new London terminus might be sited. One Frank Crocker was convinced that the location was going to be at Maida Vale, and built a stylish hotel to service it. He is reported to have jumped to his death after the railway passed it by. The building, however, now a pub called Crocker's Folly, is still in business.

The Great Central operated well until, like all railways, it was taken over by the Government for war service in 1914. After that, it suffered the fate of almost all the independent railway companies, with the Grouping Act of 1921. It then became part of the LNER, under its new Superintendent, Nigel Gresley.

CHAPTER FIFTEEN

Kent and East Sussex Railway

'They've done it out well,' said one man after looking around the Kent and East Sussex Railway complex at Tenterden. And they have – the feeling of an 'old-time' country railway is certainly there. The efforts of the staff are matched by the keen interest of the many visitors. Four or five engines may be in steam on one day, making a great show.

The biggest locos may not be able to make the sharp curves and tough gradients, but the tanks and medium-sized engines give of their best. The old Stroudley Terrier engine, No. 32650, stands proudly in the station. It worked the K & ES long before the preservation days, and is awaiting its time to come back.

Another Terrier – No. 2678 (formerly London Brighton & South Coast Railway 'Knowle') – made a comeback in 1999. This diminutive engine headed the last BR passenger train to run on the line, and previously worked on the Isle of Wight, as well as the K&ESR.

The line was originally built in the late 1890s for the Rother Valley Railway, by Colonel H. Stephens, who set up the railway according to the Light Railways Act of the time. 'Light' was the operative word, with lightly laid track serving remote villages. After 1904, it was taken over by the K&ES Joint Railway, when the northern section to Headcorn Junction was opened. The line then linked the cross-country South Eastern and Chatham line at Headcorn with Robertsbridge, on the London to Hastings main line.

In preservation, it is the aim of the K&ESR to maintain the image of Colonel Stephens' railway as far as possible. The numbers of passengers carried now is far in excess of those carried previously, so much upgrading has had to be done.

In the early days, when the preservation society was set up, the hope was to reopen the line complete. However, the obstacles were

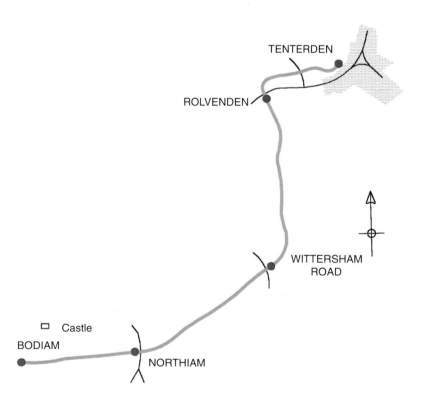

P Class No. 1556, once owned by the Mill at Robertsbridge.

too great, with the proposed A21 Robertsbridge by-pass cutting off the western end, and the whole route containing so many level crossings. Planning consents were hard to come by and, after thirteen years of struggle, the society had to settle for just the one-mile section from Tenterden to Rolvenden. With foresight, however, the railway had purchased the trackbed on to Bodiam, and always maintained the ambition to go right on to Robertsbridge.

The line was closed by British Railways in 1954 for passenger services, although it was kept open for freight until 1961. It was then reopened by the preservation society in 1975, and Northiam was reached in 1990.

Before the line closed, there was one week in 1953 when only 118 passengers used the railway. The total service for that week was 90 trains, so the figures speak for themselves. Perhaps it is not surprising that people used alternative transport – Rolvenden Station is a mile and a half from the village, and Wittersham Road Station is some 2 miles (3km) from Wittersham. (It was customary to add 'Road' after a name when a station was an embarrassing distance from the village it served.) The old railway always lost money, and many schemes had to be invented, in order to cut costs. At one time in the 1920s Colonel Stephens had used road buses on the line, linked back to back with flanged wheels. All these absurd schemes add to the charm of the railway's history. The preservationists' aim

Former L&NWR balcony coach restored by the highly skilled volunteer coach-builders at the Tenterden carriage works. The historic six-wheeled coach is turned out in early LMS colours, and a ride in it at the end of a train is a unique experience.

Part of the Victorian set of carriages restored at Tenterden.

History Note – The 'Light' Railways

The Light Railways Act of 1896 was set up to encourage and give financial incentives for the building of railways to serve thinly populated areas. This attracted entre-preneurs, and new railways duly started appearing. As they were built as cheaply as possible, they mostly avoided villages altogether, going directly between two of them. River valleys were followed wherever possible, avoiding the construction of cuttings and embankments. Even where earthworks were essential, they were often skimped on. Stations would be simple timber structures, and the simplest way to cross open roads was by ungated level crossings. It was not surprising that a proliferation of 'whistle' signs would adorn the sides of the track. The railways were run on a shoestring, and the trains were often made up of a mixture of little carriages, with a couple of trucks added for good measure.

The best exponent of these railways, involved in seventeen of them, was Colonel H. Stephens, who made light railways his life's work. The Stroudley 'Terrier' was his favoured engine, and he was constantly borrowing them from one railway to help out another. As a result, most of them have a 'much-travelled' history.

The best fingerboards in the business are at the K&ESR.

A penny platform-ticket machine – one of these would have been in every booking hall in the country.

Essential maintenance must be carried out regularly to keep the trains running efficiently. The main works are carried out here at Rolvenden.

The former South Eastern and Chatham Railway (Chilham) signal box, now sited at Tenterden Station.

In the days of the original railway the line had numerous ungated level crossings. Every one of them would have demanded a 'whistle' from the engine as it appraoched.

to maintain this spirit; after all, this is the only one of Colonel Stephens' lines to have been saved.

As well as the continuous improvement of stock and track, passenger comforts and facilities have to be catered for. The Tenterden site has children's facilities and an impressive museum depicting the life and work of Colonel Stephens.

A heritage lottery grant has been obtained in order to complete the Bodiam extension. The attraction and commercial benefits of reaching the National Trust property of Bodiam Castle are immense, with the original station still in place at Bodiam.

As it is the aim of the railway to retain the 'Light' image, the society has made a speciality of restoring and running old wooden coaches. A purpose-made workshop was specially built for this at Tenterden, in which a succession of old Victorian coaches have been restored back to their original condition. The result of this application of old-time skills and crafts-manship, by some very dedicated people, is there for all to see, and to ride in. On certain days the workshops are open to the public.

To cope with the demands of a very frequent service, a rake of ex-BR Mk. 1 coaches have been acquired. In carmine and cream, they also give an additional 'period' image to the line.

For the future, as well as the extension to Bodiam, a separate company has been set up to look into all aspects of completing the final extension to Robertsbridge. Much of the trackbed has fallen into private hands, and there is the knotty problem of crossing the A21, but the chance of linking up with Network Southeast at Robertsbridge Station is too tempting. There is even a bay platform waiting.

Enjoying a sojourn on the K&ESR, Ivatt No. 46443 climbs away from Rolvenden and approaches the Cranbrook Road crossing.

Right: **Terrier No. 32650, built in 1887, in BR livery at Tenterden Station. Out of service for many years awaiting overhaul and the issue of a ten-year boiler certificate, the engine will surely be double heading with its sister No. 2678 in the near future.**

Left: **The 'Norwegian' climbs the Tenterden Bank with a full complement of Victorian coaches.**

The P Class No. 1556 sits quietly after being taken out of service.

Returned to service after a major overhaul, Terrier SR No. 2678 approaches Tenterden Station on 31 May 1999.

A typical scene from the steam era. Visiting the railway, Ivatt Mogul BS Class 2 No. 46443 waits in the loop at Rolvenden for the Victorian train to pass through.

The 'Norwegian' at Tenterden, with the P class No. 1556 acting as pilot. Built in Sweden in 1919, and having worked in various parts of Norway, No. 376 was acquired by the K&ESR in 1971, and now performs regularly with the Victorian set.

CHAPTER SIXTEEN

Bo'ness and Kinneil Railway

The pride of Scottish preservation, the Bo'ness and Kinneil Railway is located on the southern side of the Firth of Forth at Borrowstounness. The railway was set up by the Scottish Railway Preservation Society, which set out in 1961 to save, restore and exhibit as much as possible of Scotland's railway history. By starting so promptly, after the decline of steam, the society was able to salvage a notable collection of locomotives, carriages and wagons.

Until 1979, most of the society's storage facilities were at Falkirk. Afterwards, they were able to move to Bo'ness, where there was a real possibility not only to store and exhibit, but also to run a preserved railway. Having built up a fine collection of engines and rolling stock, all their efforts could be directed towards rebuilding the line and the stations.

The complex at Bo'ness was built up from a 'green-field' site, with most of the buildings having been obtained from disused railways around Scotland. The station building was formerly at Wormit, on the south side of the Tay Bridge. The overall station roof and columns came complete from the terminus station at Edinburgh Haymarket. Built in 1842 by the Edinburgh and Glasgow Railway, it had remained intact until the 1980s, when it was dismantled by the preservation society and transported to Bo'ness. The wrought- and cast-iron footbridge came from Murthly, near Perth. The signal box was built in 1899, for the Caledonian Railway, and came from Garnqueen South Junction, just north of Coatbridge.

In 1981, the preserved railway was able to get under way. Although the infrastructure had been set up, the service initially ran from Lows Crossing, near the old Custom House, first to Kinneil Halt, and then to the new station at Birkhill. It was not until the late 1980s that the rebuilt station was ready at Bo'ness. This was not on the site of the original Bo'ness Station, but about a half a mile (1km) to the east.

At present, the track runs on past Birkhill, for about a mile, and connects with the main line at Manuel. The society has now obtained approvals and finance to extend the railway along this section, and a new terminus station will be required. There will be much work to be done, including tree clearance and the

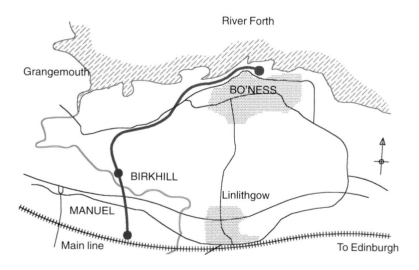

LNER Class Y9 0-4-0 saddle tank dating from 1887 on show at the Bo'ness museum.

erection of fencing. Birkhill Station will also need some modification, as it will need to become a crossing point for trains. The running of two trains increases the scope of the railway considerably.

The present end station, Birkhill, is completely new. There was never a station there in former days. It now has the added attraction of being next to the Birkhill Fireclay Mine. Set in the side of a gorge, the mine was an integral part of the Industrial Revolution because, without firebricks, there could never have been steam engines.

In the early 1800s, until the arrival of the railway, the port of Bo'ness was in decline, having lost out to Grangemouth and its newly built canal.

When the railway arrived, local coal mining was able to expand, together with other industries, and the whole area was enlivened. The new Edinburgh to Glasgow line, however, bypassed the town and, when the Bo'ness line opened in 1851, it did not connect with it. At first the Bo'ness line was freight only, but a passenger service started in 1856, and in 1865 it was taken over by the North British Railways Co.

The Caledonian Railway 0-4-4 Caley tank under repair at Bo'ness. It will not be long before No. 419 has a new ten-year certificate, and is seen heading the Bo'ness Caledonian set of carriages along the railway.

The decline of the port and railway started after the First World War, and with the ever-increasing use of road traffic, both were effectively closed in 1956. Some freight was still carried on the railway until 1965, but in the end the only section of line still used was between Kinneil and Manuel. Ironically, this was the first section of line to have opened in 1851.

The whole of the Bo'ness site deserves exploration by a visitor, as it is constantly developing. Behind the signal box is the old Bo'ness harbour, which was once thriving, but is now silted up. The export of coal was the port's main function, and the museum exhibits many relics of this industry, including a coal truck with solid wooden (dumb) buffers. These were condemned in the 1880s as being highly dangerous, and sprung buffers were introduced. The truck also has end doors where the truck would have been hoisted and tipped to discharge its load straight into the hold of a ship.

Towards the 1900s, due to the railway, many improvements were made to the Bo'ness harbour. Coal, ironworks, chemicals and saw milling were industries using the port.

On the right, just across the footbridge, is a bothy, a shepherd's mountain retreat. This one

---

History Note – Scottish Railways

The railways put the previously isolated country of Scotland in touch with the south. They also connected the ports with the cities, helping industry to expand. Work and wealth were created, and the movement of goods to England brought new opportunities. The Industrial Revolution was under way.

In this climate of economic boom, an accumulation of railway companies were set up, all privately owned. The Caledonian and the North British became the most famous, and were deadly rivals. Numerous other companies included the Glasgow and South Western Railway, the Great North of Scotland Railway and Highland Railway. Examples of rolling stock from all of these companies can be seen at the Bo'ness exhibition.

The North British Railway was the last lap for the east-coast route to Scotland, while the Caledonian stretched down to Carlisle, and took the west-coast trains through to Glasgow

and Aberdeen. The rivalry was at its most intense during the 'races to the north' (*see* page 36), when both sides headed for Kinnabar Junction in the run to Aberdeen.

Locomotives were built in Scotland, most famously at the Neilson, Hyde Park works in Glasgow, and at the Caledonian's own St Rollox works. Glasgow was known as the 'Workshop of the Empire', with a mass of industry based there. The locomotive builders were prolific exporters, with a combined total of over 4,000 locomotives exported between the 1850s and the 1930s. The Andrew Barclay works at Kilmarnock also left its mark as a leading industrial engine producer, with many examples of its little workhorses surviving into preservation.

All the railway companies had their own distinctive liveries – the North British was brown, the Highland Railway yellow, and the Caledonian blue.

came from Dunfermline, and it is now the office for the goods yard.

The museum houses the Scottish Railway Exhibition, the extensive collection of locomotives and rolling stock representing all of Scottish railway history. Informative notices give an insight into the workings of each exhibit. Many organizations across Scotland have given financial support to the exhibition, including the Scottish Tourist Board and Falkirk District Council, which from day one recognized the potential of the site and railway as the main tourist attraction of the area.

The SRPS operates in conjunction with the Glasgow Museum of Transport and other heritage centres, in providing restoration and operation facilities, with outside working a priority when possible.

Heritage and lottery grants are now being sought to fund other areas around the Bo'ness site. With every year that passes, the scene changes.

Seen across the Firth of Forth from the Old Kirk Church, 'Maude' heads a train westwards out of Bo'ness passing the site of the original Bo'ness Station.

North British Railways No. 673 'Maude' facing the signal box that was commissioned in 1999.

No. 3 'Lady Victoria' standing at Bo'ness Station. The NCB engine was built by the Andrew Barclay Company of Kilmarnock in 1916, for initial use by the Ministry of Munitions at Georgetown, Paisley.

Passing Low's Crossing, the train heads out of Bo'ness. High in the background is Bo'ness Old Kirk Church.

Poster for the Bo'ness and Kinneil Railway.

No. 673 'Maude' being prepared for duties at Bo'ness. The engine, built by Neilson's in 1891, underwent rebuilding in 1915. It was then sent on war duties, and named on its return after General Maude.

Saxa Salt 10-ton covered wagon from the Middlewich Salt Co. Ltd.

'Maude' and ex-NCB East Fife shunting engine Number 19 at Bo'ness.

The oldest locomotive of the Bo'ness collection, 0-4-0 No. 13 'Kelton Fell', built by Neilson's of Glasgow (later the North British Works) in 1876 for the Baird mines in Cumbria.

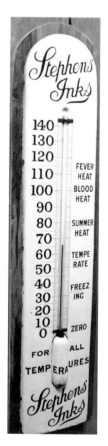

Victorian vending machine at Bo'ness station.

Above: **Wagon from the Carron Company on show at the Bo'ness Museum. Note the 'dumb' buffers, which were outlawed in the 1880s, but continued in existence until about 1920.**

A great surge of passengers for a children's event is a problem for all preserved railways. Birkhill experiences this whenever there is a special event such as a Teddy Bears' picnic.

CHAPTER SEVENTEEN

Gloucestershire Warwickshire Railway

Passing through the delightful and scenic Cotswold countryside, the Gloucestershire Warwickshire Railway is another ambitious project. With 6 miles (10km) of working track at present, all its thoughts are turned to expansion, south to Cheltenham, and north to Stratford upon Avon. This would make the line the longest in British preservation, at 25 miles (40km). The railway already own 13 miles (21km) of trackbed between Broadway and Cheltenham.

Currently, all efforts are being put into laying track, and all the takings from ticket sales are being channelled into this.

At present, the railway runs along very nicely. In an effort to maintain the image of the old Great Western Railway, it has adopted the initials GWR in its title. Every year, a major attraction is brought in from another railway to supplement the Gloucestershire Warwickshire's own stock. The railway has nine engines of its own, but only two are operational, so there is much for the volunteers to do.

The railway's headquarters is at the spacious site of Toddington. As well as the station and restaurant facilities, there are workshops, a maintenance depot and extensive sidings, and events are regularly organized. Particularly popular are Toddington's 'Thomas' days. The site is shared with a narrow-gauge railway, called the North Gloucestershire Railway. This is open most weekends, offering a ride on a different type of railway, and a variety of rare locomotives are used.

Winchcombe is the mid-station on the route. It was almost completely flattened by BR after closure, and it took some very dedicated work by the volunteers to rebuild it. The present station building came from Monmouth. It was dismantled stone by stone from its original site, and re-erected at Winchcombe in exactly its original form. The same thing had to be done for the signal box, which came from Hall Green in Birmingham.

Originally, the line was part of the Birmingham to Cheltenham route, which was built in the early 1900s as a main line. However, it gradually lost traffic to the more westerly Midland line running through Worcester. When the time came for railway rationalization, it finally lost out altogether,

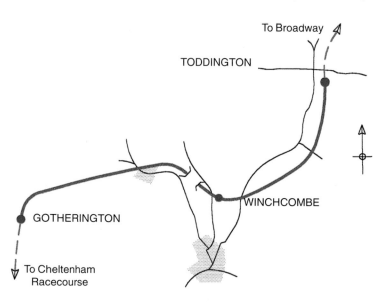

and closed in 1977. By that time it was mostly just being used as a relief line.

After closure, all the track was lifted, but this did not deter the people who had set their sights on preservation. A public company was formed, to set up fund-raising options, resulting in the purchase of the Broadway to Cheltenham trackbed. The new railway opened in 1984; it was just a quarter of a mile long, but it was a start.

Onwards from Winchcombe the line passes through the 693-yard curved Greet Tunnel, the second longest double-bore tunnel in British preservation (the longest is on the Bluebell line). After the tunnel, the track extends to Gotherington, which is the temporary end of the line.

The trackbed does not stop there, but continues right into Cheltenham. Before too long the railway should be up and running through to the station at Cheltenham Racecourse, where the platforms and station building are still intact. Hopefully, racegoers will soon be able to travel to the races at Cheltenham by steam train.

Railtrack is now showing interest in the Cheltenham to Stratford line as a possible relief route for freight. If this development continues, the GWR may even get a connection with the Birmingham to Gloucester main line.

Hunslet Austerity 'Sir Robert Peel' about to depart from Toddington. The East Lancs. engine has subsequently been sold to the Chinnor and Princes Risborough Railway to become its resident working locomotive.

Bridge loading notice.

A severe warning to boys.

Great Western Castle Class 4-6-0

The Castle Class was introduced in 1923 to supersede the Star Class. A more powerful engine was required, and the famous Churchward design was continued. The four cylinders and huge driving wheels provided all the power necessary to haul the holiday trains westward.

A firm favourite with most GWR supporters, the engines had copper and brass embellishments added to the chrome green finish, and were a delight. Their classic curved nameplates displayed the names of British castles (until these had all been used, when other titles had to be adopted). A total of 167 of the class were produced, and they were a spotter's top target. Manufacture continued until after nationalization, with previously placed orders being fulfilled.

One of the class, No. 4073 'Caerphilly Castle', together with LNER's 'Flying Scotsman', was on display at the British Empire Exhibition at Wembley in 1924. The Castle had a notice on it claiming that it was Britain's most powerful locomotive. This did not go down well with the LNER camp, and a challenge was set up for an exchange of engines to run on each other's lines. A Castle, No. 4079 'Pendennis Castle', moved to run over the former Great Northern track between King's Cross and Doncaster, while No. 4474 'Victor Wild' passed to the GWR to run between Paddington and Plymouth.

The outcome was that the Castle made better comparative times over a two-week period, and also had a lower coal consumption. This result opened the eyes of the other companies, and the Castle became the yardstick against which the design and performance of all locos were based.

'Thomas' and friend 'Robert Peel' await to lead off another trip up the line – a marvellous treat for children.

No trespassing in two languages.
Line-side signage courtesy of Winchcombe Railway Museum.

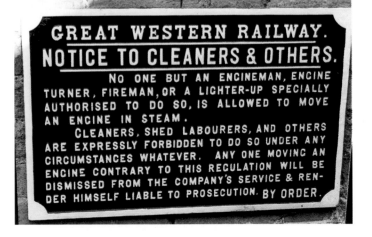

This time a warning to staff.

To a loud fanfare of whistles, steam and smoke, a Thomas event gets under way at Toddington. The engine assisting 'Thomas' is the 1936-built Hunslet No. 4 'Robert Nelson'.

'Clun Castle' double-heading out of Toddington with visiting Prairie tank No. 4566.

The Great Western Railway were happy to stamp their logo on everything from silverware to the station bench.

With the Cotswold escarpment in the background, 'Clun Castle' steams freely with a southbound train.

An authentic railway scene, with 'Clun Castle' coming out of service at Toddington.

CHAPTER EIGHTEEN

Buckingham Railway Centre

The parallel running of two steam hauled trains is the highlight of the Steam on the Met event. The two trains head out from Harrow on the Hill station at the start of the day to take up positions for single running between Amersham and Watford. Approaching Pinner, on the left is 'Black 5' No. 45110, and on the right Maunsell Mogul SR U Class No. 31625.

The Great Central Railway met with the Metropolitan Railway at Quainton Road, in Buckinghamshire. The Great Central, having been granted a joint running facility over the Metropolitan tracks, was then able to complete its London connection, and opened for passenger traffic in 1899. (For details of the original Great Central Railway, *see* Chapter 14.)

When the London Preservation Society, which had amassed a large collection of railway cast-offs in the early 1960s, was looking for a home to set up a railway centre, it found the large site at Quainton Road very suitable. The old Great Central lines had been removed in 1967, leaving a line for use just by freight traffic. From its new location the

society was to build a natural affinity with the Metropolitan and its history. Many other groups, which had 'saved' items, were also glad to make their base on the site.

In the sleepy rural Buckinghamshire countryside, the Buckingham Railway Centre's development had always been slow. That is not to detract, however, from the work of a very talented group of volunteers, who have carried out some very special renovations, and then seen their end product go off and work on the main line.

The Quainton Road centre was the care home of GWR No. 6024 'King Edward I'. This famous engine had been languishing at the Barry scrapyard for eleven years before being rescued and brought to Buckinghamshire. After all that time exposed to sea air it was very much in 'Barry condition', with much of its sheet metalwork reduced to lace. The preservationists put in sixteen years of work to complete the engine restoration, and 'King Edward I' now operates from the Didcot Railway Centre, partaking regularly in national rail tours.

As well as many renowned locomotives, a significant amount of rolling stock has also been restored at the Quainton Road centre. The Underground Railway Rolling Stock Society has made its base there and has brought along some historic Metropolitan Line carriage sets.

Pride of the former Metropolitan Railway stock is the E Class 0-4-4T No.1. This engine was built in 1898 and performed on the Aylesbury to London route before larger

engines, and then electrification, took over. After this, it was in service in the outer reaches of the line. It is the only survivor of a class of seven engines, and has been maintained to mainline standards. Now No.1 has to wait its turn for an overhaul and a new ten-year running certificate. The engine should be able to make a re-run in the year 2004, to celebrate the centenary of the opening of the Harrow to Uxbridge branch, which No.1 performed all that time ago amid much pomp and ceremony.

Nowadays, some very robust management has led the Buckingham Railway Centre to make some great advances. With the help of a lottery grant, some former storage buildings were acquired, and a new visitor centre has been completed. A former LNWR station from Rewley Road, Oxford, has been re-erected on the site to make an impressive new entrance. Behind this is a concourse, a restaurant and a new museum.

These developments have raised the status of the BRC, and the aim now is to move into the big league of heritage centres, and establish a programme of high-profile events. Already attendances at steam special days have been encouraging, and it will surely not be long before the site is one of Britain's leading rail centres.

The ex-South African Railways locomotive, which has been donated to the centre and awaits restoration. It is the largest steam locomotive in Britain, built at the North British Works, Glasgow, in 1954, and will be some sight in full steam heading a train at speed.

Pannier L99 (GWR No. 7715) operating steam rides at Quainton Road on a stormy but sunny September day in 1999.

Little 0-4-0 Industrial Engines

The little steam engines that used to shunt around sites such as docks, shipyards and factories have languished for a long time at the back of steam centres. They are now starting to be appreciated. Although they are not strong enough to run with passenger trains for any distance, they make an ideal secondary attraction around a main area. Not to be confused with the slightly bigger 'austerity-type' tanks, these little 'redoubtables' offer a low-budget alternative as a restoration project.

Made by such companies as Peckett, Hunslet, Andrew Barclay, Sentinel and North British, these engines were unsung workhorses. They had to be quick to fire up, easy to get into reverse, and able to operate on very bad track with very sharp curves and gradients. Usually operated by one man, they would often receive the minimum of maintenance, and be used relentlessly. Many companies, however, respected them, and kept them very smart, seeing them as an external showpiece to their works.

The Quainton Road centre has a remarkable set of these engines on their books, and these are now creating much interest.

'Steam on the Met'

The 'Steam on the Met' event was started in 1989 as a one-off to celebrate the centenary of the opening of the Chesham branch. It was so successful that it became a regular feature of the steam calendar.

The showpiece at the start of each day is the parallel running of two trains. This is usually from Harrow-on-the-Hill to Amersham, and then there is a scheduled steam-hauled service, with two trains running between Amersham and Watford. It is a chance for enthusiasts to ride behind a steam train, and then to view a train from a variety of locations across London's Metroland.

Four engines took part in the 1999 event, one from each region of the former 'Big Four' railway companies. On the backs of the trains, to provide air-braking, were a Class 20 diesel, and one of the Metropolitan electric locomotives, 'Sarah Siddons'. These were popular in their day, and it is a delight to see them in action. The Metropolitan No.1 E Class engine was on static display at Rickmansworth during the event.

The centre is divided by a Railtrack goods line. The small industrial locos are stored on the down side. In the distance is the down-yard restoration building.

Quainton Road was the station that was at one time the link to the Great Central Railway.

Pannier L99 (GWR No. 7715) operating steam rides at Quainton Road.

CHAPTER NINETEEN

Isle of Wight Steam Railway

In order to visit the Isle of Wight Steam Railway, non-holidaymakers do have to make a special effort, but this is easy enough to do. For about £13, a ticket can be obtained from the Wight-Link Ferry Company at Portsmouth Harbour, providing the ferry crossing, travel on the Island Line Railway, and unlimited travel on the steam railway.

The Island Line runs from Ryde Pier Head through to Shanklin, and with a stop at Smallbrook junction, there will be a steam train waiting. Londoners will feel quite at home on the Island Line, as it is electrified and the rolling stock consists of ex-Bakerloo Line tube trains.

Once aboard the steam train, the visitor is back in a bygone age. The Victorian and

Edwardian carriages are usually hauled by one of the two Stroudley Terriers owned by the railway. The tight timetable allows the trains to work briskly, and they provide a very pleasant experience for passengers as they hurry along.

The railway's headquarters and main centre is at Havenstreet. This is the best access point for car travellers, with free parking, a picnic area and a caravan and camping site. The facilities are outstanding, with a restaurant, bookshop, museum, original SR station and signal cabin, works area and engine shed. The bookshop and museum are housed in an interesting small Victorian former gas factory, which blends ideally into the railway scene.

In 1966, BR steam came to an end on the island. The 7½-mile (12km) line between Ryde Pier and Shanklin was electrified and adapted to suit the ex-London Transport tube trains.

At the turn of the 1900s, a string of short railways owned by different companies criss-crossed the island. These became constituents of the Southern Railway in 1923, at the time of Grouping. The closures started in the 1950s, with first the Ventnor West branch, then the Bembridge and Freshwater tracks, and then the Newport to Sandown line, in 1956. What remained, including the route of the IoWSR, succumbed shortly after that. With the increase in car ownership, it was typical of the decline in railways everywhere. The Shanklin to Ventnor section was the last to close, in April 1966, leaving just the one line, to Ryde Pier, which was electrified in 1967.

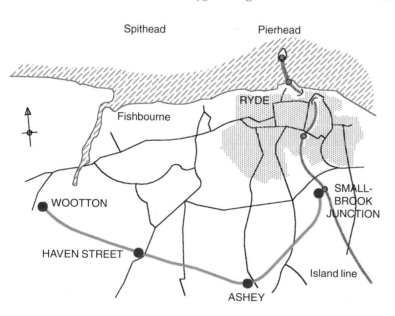

The visiting E4 Class, on loan from the Bluebell Railway, heading a train at Smallbrook Junction.

A group of enthusiasts formed the Wight Locomotive Society in 1966, with the aim of preserving a section of island railway as a steam railway. They purchased the ex-LSWR 0-4-4 tank No. 24 'Calbourne', together with five of the island's historic carriages, and they were almost in business. A lease was obtained for the line between Wooton and Smallbrook,

but progress was slow, and it was not until 1991 that the full 5 miles (8km) were in operation.

As with all preserved railways, one eye is always kept on possible expansions. With the eastern end meeting the electrified line, only a short addition would be possible – to Ryde, St Johns Road Station. There is no chance of

Terrier No. 11 (BR 32640) 'Newport' in position at Havenstreet to take the next service to Smallbrook Junction.

passing the Ryde tunnel beyond this, as its height was raised to avoid flooding, and it now suits only the tube trains.

There may, however, be some chance of a western extension to Newport. Although the original trackbed now has too many obstructions, a new route has been identified. If a successful heritage lottery grant could be obtained, there might be a real chance for the future.

The Stroudley Terriers

Nine of these diminutive engines survive in preservation, all dating from between 1872 and 1880. They were first designed for the East London Railway, and built at Brighton. It is a tribute to the class, and a sign of its success, that so many have survived.

When the Light Railways Act of 1896 was introduced, a flurry of line-building activity followed, and the small powerful Terriers were able to show their true worth. The popular Stroudley Terrier was also used on many lines where weight restrictions were critical, such as the former Havant to Hayling Island branch, with the severly restricted Langstone Bridge.

Of the nine survivors, two are with the Bluebell Railway – BR No. 32636 'Fenchurch' and No. 32655 'Stepney'. The Isle of Wight Steam Railway also has two – BR No. 32646

'Freshwater' and BR No. 32640 'Newport'. The Kent and East Sussex Railway has three – BR No. 32670 'Bodiam', BR No. 32650 'Sutton' and BR No. 32678 'Knowle'. The final Terrier is the former LBSCR No. 82 'Boxhill', which is in the National Railway Museum collection.

All of these engines have interesting histories. They have appeared in different guises with the changes in railway operation over the years. Many have been left idle in later life, which has resulted in most of their vital components deteriorating. Replacing the major components has proved very expensive. The IoWSR and the K&ESR have sensibly collaborated in ordering new boilers from the same manufacturer; in this way, common costs are shared, as such jobs as 'tooling up' are done only once.

A clear warning for the unwary.

The visiting E4 0-6-2T No. 473 'Birch Grove' stands at Havenstreet Station during the steam festival on 21 August 1999.

These tiny engines make a fascinating sight when they are doubled up. The pairing here is Stroudley Terrier No.8 'Freshwater' and O2 Class No.24 'Calbourne' (built 1891), preparing to take one of the services at the August 1999 steam festival.

Period carriage stock in use at Havenstreet finished in Southern green livery.

Examples from the ex-London Transport tube train system were acquired for use on the island's electric railway. Here, one of the ex-Bakerloo Line stock approaches Smallbrook Junction.

The mascots Stroudley and Billington keep an eye on proceedings at Havenstreet.

Stroudley Terrier No. 11 heads a train at Smallbrook Junction after picking up passengers from the connecting electric trains on the Ryde to Shanklin line.

E4 Class 'Birch Grove', visiting the IoWSR in August 1999, the largest loco ever to visit the railway and just about the biggest that it could accommodate. Here, it is running round the train at Smallbrook Junction.

CHAPTER TWENTY

Midland Railway Centre

The approach point to the Midland Railway Centre for cars is the sleepy station of Butterley, near Ripley in Derbyshire, just beside the reservoir. At first sight, little is seen of the complex, which lies half a mile down the line, although the east-west route of the line provides fine photographic opportunities across the water. A train ride or a walk down a designated route takes the visitor to the museum complex at Swanwick Junction. This is the heart of the railway and covers a site of 23 acres. Access to the site by car is difficult (directions available from the bookshop at Butterley Station). A family can be easily entertained at Swanwick Junction for a whole day. There are children's activities, model, miniature and narrow-gauge railways, as well as an animal farm and a Victorian street scene.

The railway has the biggest collection of diesel locomotives in Britain. They are all on show at the centre in various states of restoration. A new diesel depot is being erected to do justice to the collection, and to ensure the finest maintenance facilities.

A big exhibition hall specializes in showing historic Midland Railway locomotives, carriages and wagons. There is even a fireless locomotive from the Boots chemical works. One special exhibit is the 1866-built Kirtley 2-4-0 engine No. 158A, built at Derby for mainline work to London King's Cross. (The Midland Railway used its rival's station until it was able to build its own, St Pancras, in 1868.)

Pride of the railway are the exhibits in the West Shed. This is the home of the Princess Royal Class 46203 'Princess Margaret Rose'

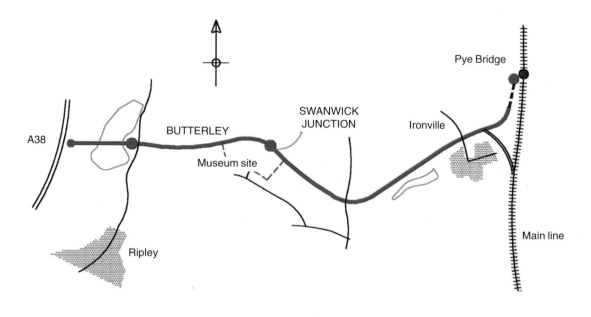

The 4MT Standard tank engine No. 80080 awaits departure from Butterley Station with a scheduled service.

The friends of the railway play their part by dressing up for a Victorian event. The train with Jinty No. 47327 at the head waits at Butterley Station.

The Princess Royal Class 4-6-2

The Princess Royal Class was the first of William Stanier's attempts to develop a large engine to rival Gresley's LNER and its A Class. The aim was to produce an engine that could do the 400-mile (640-km) London to Glasgow run without an engine change.

The previous top-link engines of the LMS were the 'Royal Scots'. They were solid performers, but after about 300 miles (480km) the firebox would be choked with ashes and clinker. This meant that, on the northern run, an engine change was always necessary at Carlisle.

Stanier was taking no chances with the 'Princess Royals', which were given a huge firegrate totalling 45 sq ft. Also with the addition of a massive boiler, these engines had a formidable appearance, being the longest in the country.

A total of twelve were built, the first two in 1933, followed by a further ten in 1935. No. 6203 'Princess Margaret Rose' was part of the 1935 batch.

It is recorded that, on 16 November 1936, 6201 'Princess Elizabeth' covered the London Euston to Glasgow run of 401 miles (642km) in 5 hours, 53 minutes.

and 46233 'Duchess of Sutherland'. These magnificent locomotives are always receiving great care and attention. A colossal amount of time and money has to be spent to get these machines certified for mainline use.

'Princess Margaret Rose' finished a mainline running programme in 1991, and now awaits her turn for overhaul, and a new ten-year certificate. It is interesting to see from the history notes displayed beside the engine that it ran with four different liveries during its working life: Crimson Lake, Black, Caledonian Blue and BR Brunswick Green.

The 'Duchess' has just undergone a full overhaul, with a heritage lottery grant of £325,000 being put towards the costs. The boiler was sent to the Severn Valley Railway's enginee-ring workshop at Bridgnorth for specialist repair. Wheels, frame and all mechanical parts have received meticulous attention, and the whole overhaul took only eighteen months. The 'Duchess of Sutherland' had not been steamed since 1974, when it was in the care of the Bressingham Steam Museum. It is the only one of the three preserved Coronation Pacifics not to have originally been streamlined.

The Princess Royal Class Locomotive Trust's pride and joy, in the LMS crimson lake livery, No. 46203 'Princess Margaret Rose' awaits an overhaul and another run out on the main line with a steam special.

The entrance sign to the famous West Shed.

The huge 'Princess Margaret Rose' stands in the West Shed at the Swanwick Junction site. In the foreground are the wheels of the Coronation Class No. 46233 'Duchess of Sutherland'.

The wheels and frame of No. 46233 'Duchess of Sutherland' are being refurbished at the Midland Centre, while the return of the boiler is awaited from the Bridgnorth Machine Shop on the Severn Valley Railway.

Acting as good support for the main feature of the day. The little 0-4-0 shunting engine chuffs around the sidings at Swanwick Junction.

British Standard 4MT Class No. 80080 heads an eastbound train past Butterley Reservoir.

CHAPTER TWENTY ONE

Didcot Railway Centre

Didcot Railway Centre is situated right next to Didcot Parkway mainline station, on the route of Brunel's original London to Bristol broad-gauge railway, and in the heart of Great Western country. It is a fine place to show off the best of the GWR.

Although the centre is fairly compact, there is enough in the 16-acre site to keep a visitor interested for many hours. There is something for everyone – the engine sheds and workshops, the museum and bookshop, or a ride on a period branch-line train. There is also a second stretch of line where a ride can be taken in a train hauled by a classic Great Western engine, or a special visiting locomotive.

In a livery of wartime black, heavy freight loco No. 3822 2-8-0 (built in 1940) is shown here on the main display line at Didcot.

The centre now has its own impressive collection of locos and rolling stock restored by its own members, but other owners of historic GWR locomotives also have their prized possessions housed and steamed at Didcot.

The area at the north end of the site is of special interest. Here, an example of 1880s broad-gauge workings has been assembled, together with authentic signalling. Some genuine old broad-gauge rails, which were discovered buried near Burlescombe in Devon, have been donated and used. They have been laid to exhibit dual-gauge workings – that is to say, broad and standard gauge on the same trackbed. This difficult working required three rails, and an intricate set of points, and a standard-gauge train had to change sides of the track to negotiate the points.

The lines pass into an authentic transfer shed, which was rescued from another part of Didcot. Here, trains of different gauges transfer goods from one train to another. It is worth noting the sizes of the different arches.

To control the broad-gauge workings a signal box from Frome North was acquired, and moved here by road. It has been given its original name of Frome Mineral Junction, where it controlled broad-gauge workings of coal and stone coming from the Radstock area.

A signal box from Radstock has also been rescued, and controls the standard-gauge stretch of line that runs from the transfer shed to a new station called Didcot Halt. This re-

creates a typical stretch of a 1930s branch line, complete with semaphore signalling and a level crossing, all controlled from the Radstock box. Other lineside paraphernalia completes the scene. Visitors are given a train ride either in a push-pull auto-train, or a 1930s diesel railcar.

The workings at the top end of the Didcot Centre, all put together by the volunteers of the Great Western Society, are one of the best examples of a working exhibit in Britain. The society started back in 1962, when a group of schoolboys saw an auto-train about to be discarded at Southall, and decided to try and save it. After a letter to *The Railway* magazine was published, interest was shown and donations started to come in, and the great salvage operation was under way. On the strength of that, other steam locomotives were targeted, and the Great Western

Castle Class engines on display at Didcot. No. 5051 'Earl Bathurst' and No. 4073 'Caerphilly Castle' side by side.

A study of the driving wheels and nameplate of the 'Castle'. The wheels are 6ft 8ins in diameter.

The GWR auto-train under way from the transfer shed on the short journey to Didcot Halt.

The King Class 4-6-0

The Great Western Railway did not rest on its laurels after the success of the Castle Class. With the ever-increasing holiday traffic, an even more powerful locomotive was programmed – the King.

In 1927, the first King, 'King George V', was wheeled out of the Swindon works. Owing to the curvature of many of the GWR main routes, a 4-6-0 wheel arrangement was preferred (rather than a Pacific), and the engine was the most powerful of this kind in Britain.

The weight of the engine confined it to just three routes: the London lines to Plymouth, Bristol and Wolverhampton. Only thirty were built in total, but they were the elite of the Great Western. Like the 'Castle', when the 'King' first appeared it was fitted with low-sided tenders. This caused much anguish to the GWR enthusiasts, until the matter was put right and full-sided tenders were substituted.

Society was formed. The only problem with acquiring such large items was finding somewhere to put them. The engine shed at Didcot had become disused, and, in 1967, the society was allowed to house its collection of a few carriages and three locomotives there. Since then, the dedicated work of a volunteer force has created the working museum that is seen today.

Every season, the Didcot Railway has special visiting engines on show and in steam. Here is the Merchant Navy Class No. 35028 'Clan Line' on the main demonstration line.

The auto-train headed by the specially adapted tank engine No. 1466 about to depart the transfer shed at Didcot.

The signal box that once controlled the junction of the branch to Radstock and Bristol from the main line at Frome is now preserved at Didcot.

Dual-gauge linework; the transfer shed is from the broad-gauge days, when goods would be transferred from a train of one gauge to another.

Outside the engine shed sits 'King Edward I', the most powerful class of engine on the Great Western Railway.

The magnificent nameplates of the Great Western Railway engines were the envy of every other railway.

Castle Class 4-6-0 No. 5051 'Earl of Bathurst' and V2 Class 2-6-2 No. 60800 'Green Arrow' in front of the engine shed.

The engine that was on display at the London Science Museum for thirty-five years, No. 4073 'Caerphilly Castle', en route for a home-coming to Swindon in summer 1999. Note the low-sided tender and the clerestory coaches, which would have had gas lamps inside high up in the roof space.

The inside of the transfer shed with some typical GWR exhibits, including the baggage trolleys; the raised handle means that the brake is on.

Inside the engine shed, No. 5900 'Hinderton Hall' sits quietly out of service.

No. 5051 ' Earl Bathurst' with visitor LNER V2 Class No. 60800 ' Green Arrow'.

CHAPTER TWENTY TWO

Lakeside and Haverthwaite Railway

After various attempts to obtain use of the line to Ulverston, the 3-mile (5km) preserved railway line from Haverthwaite to the Lakeside Station on the edge of Lake Windermere was opened, in 1973.

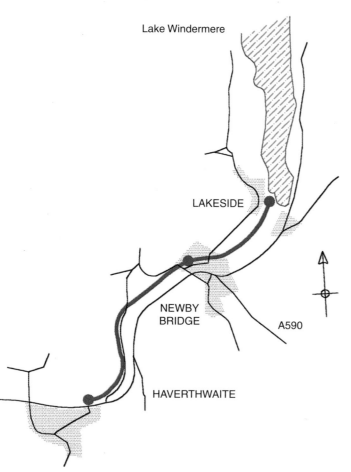

Lake Windermere

LAKESIDE

NEWBY BRIDGE

A590

HAVERTHWAITE

Dr Peter Beet, who later took over the BR Carnforth Motive Power Depot, had expressed an interest in reopening the whole 7-mile (11km) line. However, road improvements in the area made the extension impossible, and Dr Beet did not pursue his interest. The way was then clear for the establishment of the Lakeside and Haverthwaite Railway Co. Ltd.

Mr Austin Maher became the owner of the railway in 1973. After British Railways had given notice of its closure, he and his brother Charles had made a cine film from the footplate of a special steam run down the whole line. This film sparked interest in the line and generated thoughts of its possible reopening as a preserved heritage railway.

Formerly, the line was part of the Furness Railway, and its main function was the transportation of coal and iron ore and other freight to feed the industry of the area, and beyond. However, the railway was soon to recognize a profitable new opportunity. Tourism was taking off in a big way, and the Lake District was beckoning.

The Victorians' love of the railways, and their desire to travel, was soon to be exploited by the private railway companies of the region. The Furness Railway extended its line up to Lakeside, and before long it was providing a service that linked with the Windermere steamers. Today's railway does exactly the same thing – an inclusive ticket

The former War Department Hunslet Austerity engine 'Cumbria' prepares to leave Haverthwaite Station.

purchased at Haverthwaite includes a connection for a Windermere lake cruise.

A very special locomotive has now found a home at Haverthwaite. For many years, the Furness Railway locomotive No.20 had been kept at the Carnforth Steam Museum. In 1990, it was taken over by the Furness Railway Trust. A heritage lottery grant was obtained, and the locomotive was moved to Barrow for restoration. The new tender was

Britain's oldest working standard gauge steam locomotive on special display outside the engine shed at Haverthwaite.

built by students from Furness College in Barrow, aided by the study of old photographs.

No.20 is now a huge attraction at its home on the Lakeside and Haverthwaite Railway, and runs in service on the line on several dates in a season.

Brought back into service in early 1999, No.20 is now Britain's oldest working standard-gauge steam locomotive. Proudly displaying the Furness Indian Red livery, it has created interest nationwide, and was immediately invited to be a participant in the Rail 2000 Millennium Steam Cavalcade. This event will celebrate the 175th anniversary of the opening of the Stockton and Darlington Railway.

The Victorians likened No.20, built in 1863, to a 'kettle on wheels'. The locomotive spent most of its working life as a humble industrial saddle-tank, after initially working the Furness Railway as a freight locomotive. The Barrow Haematite Steel Co. purchased the engine in 1870, when its conversion took place. The engine then worked right through to 1960, and escaped the cutter's torch by being donated to stand at a local school.

Hunslet Austerity Tank 0-6-0

This class originates from a war-time design for the Ministry of Supply, which required a sturdy tank engine that would give two years' arduous service for the war effort.

Several builders were called upon for the construction, including the Hunslet Co. of Leeds. This company became the lead manufacturer and supervized the distribution of parts, which were almost in kit form.

The LNER purchased the majority of the engines after the war, and gave them a class designation of J94, which now defines the class in general.

They were, like most of the war engines, unsung heroes and production continued after the cessation of hostilities, right up until 1964. They then had the privilege of being the last steam-powered, standard-gauge locomotives built for use in Britain.

The class was to be an instant success with the coming of preservation. Many were still quite 'young', and cheap to acquire. They were the ideal engine to work the small lines, and proved to be powerful pullers, having no trouble with a five- or six-coach set.

The Lakeside and Haverthwaite Railway has two examples: 'Cumbria', which dates from 1952, and was stored for a long period at Long Marston army depot; and 'Repulse', which was built in 1950, and had a more challenging working life with the North Western Area of the National Coal Board.

'Cumbria' gets underway with the train out of Haverthwaite.

Above: **The train headed by 'Cumbria' approaches Newby Bridge.**

Below: **No. 20 makes a fine picture at Haverthwaite. It is a rare sight to see an 0-4-0 engine with a tender.**

Thanks Dai

A Tribute to Dai Woodham

The story of the late Dai Woodham and his scrapyard at Barry in South Wales is well documented, and an important part of preservation folklore.

The story started in 1959, when, hearing of the impending disposal by British Railways of all its steam locomotives, Dai and his brother turned their attention away from shipping salvage. They decided to concentrate on a potentially lucrative new market, and bought in all 297 locomotives from BR for scrapping.

As the locomotives started to come in, together with redundant carriages and trucks, the brothers began by breaking up the rolling stock as a first priority. They did cut up some of the locomotives, but fortunately the preservationists moved in before they had got around to doing too much damage. Rows and rows of decaying engines languished in the scrapyard, some of which were there for decades, being attacked by the sea air.

It was obviously better business to sell an engine whole, rather than going through the process of cutting up and disposing of piles of scrap metal. They were also sympathetic to the cause of saving these historic monsters. Dai took the prominent role in dealing with sales, and it is due to his goodwill that so many were saved. If this stock of engines had not been available, the preserved railway sites in Britain would be few and far between, and would not have developed into such a booming heritage industry.

Of the 297 engines that came through the yard, an amazing 213 were saved. There were mainly Southern, Great Western and Standard types, as well as some Midland Region stock. These are now the mainstay of the engines in use today.

The first engine to leave for preservation was a Midland 'Black Five' No. 43924, which went to Keighley. Many people grouped together to buy certain engines and form preservation societies and fund raising became the name of the game. Not only had the engine to be bought, but there were also the problems of transport, storage and restoration. It was to take much time and money. Many of the engines are still in 'Barry condition' today, but they are safe from the cutter's torch, and their turn will come.

The last engine to be removed from the yard was the GWR Prairie tank No. 5553, in January 1990. It had spent an incredible 28 years at the yard, longer than any other engine. The 2-6-2T has now been restored and is due to get a running certificate in 2000.

Dai Woodham died in 1994, and many tributes were bestowed on him in his final years. He had visited some of the preserved sites, and seen with disbelief how some of the rusting hulks from his yard had been transformed into such pristine condition.

The site at Barry Island has now been built on, and the first era of the preserved railway movement is over. We all owe thanks to Dai, and to all those people who passed through the Barry gates and came away with an engine!

Some locomotives that were rescued from the Barry scrapyard and are as yet unrestored (but safe).

A very powerful locomotive awaits restoration at the Buckingham railway Centre. The 2-8-2T GWR 72XX Class No. 7200. The engine went to Barry in 1963 and was removed in 1980.

Following a derailment at the Barry scrapyard. The wheels of GWR 'King Edward II' had to be cut away to move the engine. They are now on show at Didcot.

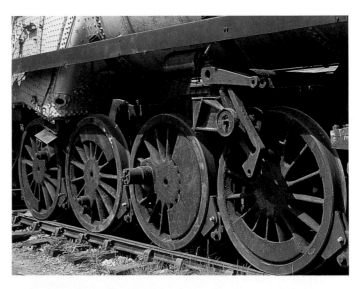

9F No. 92219 is at the Midland Railway Centre and restoration work had begun to the boiler.

At some stage the wheels of No. 92219 will need a very specialized restoration. The Midland Railway Centre have the facilities to do this.

The tender of No. 45491 stands alongside 9F No. 92219.

A closer study of the decayed metalwork of the tender of 45491.

A Black 5 awaits its restoration at the Birmingham Railway Museum.

A tender for Black 5 No. 45451. Where do you go from here, with much of the sheet metalwork reduced to lace?

Prelude to Preservation

Before the Great War, the railways were owned by hundreds of private companies. Mergers brought the number down, but the system was inefficient. The war took the railways into Government hands, but when the time came to return to privatization, something needed to be done.

The Railway 'Grouping' Bill of 1921 grouped the railways into four regional companies: the London and North Eastern (LNER), the London Midland Scottish (LMS), the Southern (SR) and the Great Western Railway (GWR) and the new companies became known as the 'Big Four' in 1923. All had main lines radiating from London terminus stations, and they covered the whole of the British mainland. A few of the old private companies, such as the Midland and Great Northern, and the Somerset and Dorset, were allowed to keep their identity, maintaining joint agreements with their neighbouring big brother.

The 'Big Four' carried the railways through until after the Second World War. All were making a loss, and the war had left the system in a dilapidated state. As a result, the railways were taken into Government ownership, with nationalization in 1948. The title 'British Railways' was introduced, and the former regional organization was maintained, with the namings being revised to Eastern (ER), Midland (MR), Southern (SR) and Western (WR). There was also separate North Eastern and Scottish Regions. Each main region maintained its colour identity from before: Eastern was blue, Midland red, Southern green, and Western brown.

British Railways set about an ambitious modernization programme including the building of a new range of twelve Standard Class locomotives. The finest of these were the Britannia Class, one of which (No. 70004 'William Shakespeare') was shown at the 1951 Festival of Britain Exhibition. The various BR Standard Classes adopted new standard colours. Passenger expresses were Brunswick green, lined with black and orange. Short-range passenger and mixed-traffic classes were black, lined with red, cream and grey. Freight and shunting engines had just an unlined black livery. All locos displayed the lion and wheel logo.

The preservation movement have locomotives and rolling stock from all periods and stock from the Grouping and nationalization periods means they have a choice of liveries. The old pre-Great War engines are featured in the colours of their former private companies.

The Standard Classes were popular with crews and maintenance staff, as they incorporated new innovations such as fully enclosed cabs, self-cleaning smoke boxes, and rocking grates for easy firebox emptying. These engines feature well in preservation, many having had only a short working life prior to the demise of steam-powered traction.

Each of the main companies had an influential Chief Mechanical Engineer, or Superintendent, all of whom became famous for the locomotives they introduced. The LNER had Gresley, Thompson and Peppercorn. The LMS had Stanier and H.G. Ivatt. Southern had Maunsell and Bulleid, and the GWR had Collett and Hawksworth following on from Churchward.

Wheel Arrangements

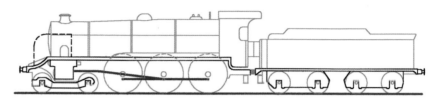

bogie	driving wheels	back	tender wheels
4	6	0	not included

General Purpose Engine – Passenger and Freight
Express Passenger

SOME TYPICAL WHEEL ARRANGEMENTS
FOR LOCOMOTIVES FEATURED IN THIS BOOK

4–6–2
Express Passenger (Pacific)

4–4–0
Express Passenger & Older Engine

2–10–0
Heavy Freight & Severe Route Passenger

0–8–0
Heavy Freight

2–8–0
Heavy Freight

0–6–0
Freight & Slow Passenger

2–6–4
B.R. Standard Class Tank

0–4–4
Tank Engine

2–6–2
Light Passenger, Suburban Traffic (Prairie)

2–6–0
Passenger & General Purpose Engine
(Mogul)

Steam Guide
(Standard Gauge)

ALDERNEY RAILWAY
Alderney
CI
Tel: 01455 634373

AVON VALLEY RAILWAY
Bitton Station
Willsbridge
Bristol
Talking timetable: 0117 932 7296
0117 932 5538

BARROW HILL ROUNDHOUSE
Chesterfield
Derbyshire
Tel: 01246 472450

BATTLEFIELD LINE
Shackerstone Station
Shackerstone
Leicestershire
Tel: 01827 880754

BIRMINGHAM RAILWAY MUSEUM
Warwick Street
Tysely
Birmingham
West Midlands
Tel: 0121 707 4696

BLUEBELL RAILWAY
Sheffield Park Station
East Sussex
Talking timetable: 01825 722370
General: 01825 723777

BODMIN AND WENFORD RAILWAY
Bodmin Gen. Station
Bodmin
Cornwall
Tel: 01208 73666

BO'NESS AND KINNEIL RAILWAY
Bo'ness Station
Bo'ness
West Lothian
Tel: 01506 822298

BOWES RAILWAY CENTRE
Gateshead
Co. Durham
Tel: 0191 416 1847

BRESSINGHAM STEAM MUSEUM
Nr Diss
Norfolk
Tel: 01379 687386

BRISTOL HARBOUR RAILWAY
Princes Wharf
Bristol
Tel: 0117 925 1470

BUCKINGHAM RAILWAY CENTRE
Quainton Road
Bucks
Talking timetable: 01296 655720

CAERPHILLY RAILWAY
Caerphilly
M. Glamorgan
Tel: 01222 888387

CALEDONIAN RAILWAY
Brechin
Angus
Talking timetable: 01356 622992
General: 01674 810318

CHASEWATER RAILWAY
Brownhills West
Walsall
West Midlands
Tel: 01543 452623

CHEDDLETON RAILWAY CENTRE
Nr Leek
Staffs
Tel: 01538 360522 / 01782 612203

CHINNOR AND PRINCES RISBOROUGH RAILWAY
Princes Risborough
Bucks
Talking timetable: 01844 353535

CHOLSEY & WALLINGFORD RAILWAY
Wallingford
Oxon
Tel: 01491 835067

CHURNET VALLEY RAILWAY
Cheddleton
Staffs
Tel: 01538 360522

COLNE VALLEY RAILWAY
Castle Hedingham
Essex
Tel: 01787 461174

COVENTRY RAILWAY CENTRE
Adj. Coventry Airport
Tel: 01455 634373

DARLINGTON RAILWAY CENTRE AND MUSEUM
Darlington
Co. Durham
Tel: 01325 460532

DEAN FOREST RAILWAY
Lydney
Glos
Talking timetable: 01594 843432
General: 845840

DERWENT VALLEY LIGHT RAILWAY
Murton
North Yorkshire
Tel: 01904 489966

DEVON RAILWAY CENTRE
Bickleigh
Tiverton
Tel: 01884 855671

DIDCOT RAILWAY CENTRE
Adj. Didcot Parkway Station
Didcot
Oxon
Tel: 01235 817200

DOWNPATRICK STEAM RAILWAY
Downpatrick Station
Co. Down
Tel: 01396 615779

EAST ANGLIAN RAILWAY MUSEUM
Chappel and Wakes Colne Station
Colchester
Essex
Tel: 01206 242524

EAST KENT RAILWAY
Shepherdswell
Kent
Tel: 01304 832042

EAST SOMERSET RAILWAY
Cranmore Railway Station
Shepton Mallet
Somerset
Tel: 01749 880417

EAST LANCASHIRE RAILWAY
Bolton Street Station
Bury
Lancs
Tel: 0161 764 7790

ELSCAR STEAM RAILWAY
(Elscar Heritage Centre)
Nr Barnsley
W. Yorks
Tel: 01226 740203

EMBSAY AND BOLTON ABBEY STEAM RAILWAY
Skipton
N. Yorks
Talking timetable: 01756 795189
General: 710614

FOXFIELD STEAM RAILWAY
Blythe Bridge
Stoke-on Trent
Tel: 01782 396210

GLOUCESTERSHIRE WARWICKSHIRE RAILWAY
Toddington
Gloucestershire
Tel: 01242 621405

GREAT CENTRAL RAILWAY
Loughborough Central Station
Leicestershire
Talking timetable: 01509 211599
General: 230726

GREAT NORTHERN RAILWAY
Ludborough
Lincolnshire
Tel: 01507 363881

GREAT WESTERN RAILWAY MUSEUM
Swindon
Tel: 01793 466555

GWILI RAILWAY
Carmarthen
Tel: 01267 230666

HOLLYCOMBE STEAM COLLECTION
Liphook
Hants
Tel: 01428 724900

ISLE OF WIGHT STEAM RAILWAY
The Railway Station
Havenstreet
IoW
Tel: 01983 882204

KEIGHLEY AND WORTH VALLEY RAILWAY
The Railway Station
Haworth
W. Yorks
Talking timetable: 01535 647777
General: 01535 645214

KENT AND EAST SUSSEX RAILWAY
Tenterden
Kent
Tel: 01580 765155

LAKESIDE AND HAVERTHWAITE RAILWAY
Haverthwaite Station
Nr Ulverstone
Cumbria
Tel: 015395 31594

LAVENDER LINE
Isfield Station
Nr Uckfield
East Sussex
Tel: 01825 750515

LLANGOLLEN RAILWAY
The Station
Abbey Road, Llangollen, Denbys
Talking timetable: 01978 860951
General: 860979

LONDON TRANSPORT MUSEUM
Covent Garden
London
Tel: 020 7379 6344

**MANGAPPS FARM RAILWAY
MUSEUM**
Burnham-on-Crouch
Essex
Tel: 01621 784898

MIDDLETON RAILWAY
The Station
Moor Road
Hunslet
Leeds
W. Yorks
Tel?

MID-NORFOLK RAILWAY
Dereham
Norfolk
Tel: 01362 690633

**MID-HANTS RAILWAY (WATERCRESS
LINE)**
The Railway Station
Alresford
Hampshire
Talking timetable: 01962 734866
General: 733810

MIDLAND RAILWAY CENTRE
Butterley Railway Station
Ripley
Derbyshire
Tel: 01773 570140

MID-SUFFOLK LIGHT RAILWAY
Wetheringsett
Suffolk
Tel: 01473 611683

MUSEUM OF TRANSPORT
Glasgow
Tel: 0141 287 2720

NATIONAL RAILWAY MUSEUM
York
Tel: 01904 621261

NENE VALLEY RAILWAY
Wansford Station
Stibbington
Peterborough
Cambs
Talking timetable: 01780 784444
General: 01580 765155

**NORTHAMPTON AND LAMPORT
RAILWAY**
Pitsford and Brampton Station
Chapel Brampton
Northants
Tel: 01604 820327

**NORTHAMPTONSHIRE IRONSTONE
RAILWAY TRUST**
Northampton
Tel: 01604 702031

NORTH NORFOLK RAILWAY
The Station
Sheringham
Norfolk
Tel: 01263 822045

NORTH TYNESIDE STEAM RAILWAY
Northshields
Tel: 0191 262 2627

NORTH YORK MOORS RAILWAY
Pickering Station
North Yorkshire
Tel: 01751 472508

NOTTINGHAM HERITAGE CENTRE
Ruddington
Notts
Tel: 0115 940 5705

PAIGNTON AND DARTMOUTH STEAM RAILWAY
Queens Park Station
Paignton
Devon
Tel: 01803 555872

PALLOT HERITAGE STEAM MUSEUM
Trinity
Jersey
Tel: 01534 865307

PEAK RAIL
Matlock
Derbyshire
Tel: 01629 580381

PONTYPOOL AND BLAENAVON RAILWAY
Blaenavon
Tel: 01495 792263

RAILWAY PRESERVATION SOCIETY OF IRELAND
Whitehead
Tel: 01960 353567

SEVERN VALLEY RAILWAY
Bewdley
Worcestershire
Talking timetable: 0800 600900
General: 01299 403816

SOUTH DEVON RAILWAY
The Station
Buckfastleigh
Devon
Tel: 01364 642338

SOUTHALL RAILWAY CENTRE
Adj. Southall Station
Southall
Middlesex
Talking timetable: 020 8574 8100
General: 020 8574 1529

SPA VALLEY RAILWAY
Tunbridge Wells
Tel: 01892 537715

STRATHSPEY RAILWAY
Aviemore
Invernesshire
Tel: 01479 810725

SWANAGE RAILWAY
Station House
Swanage
Dorset
Tel: 01929 425800

SWANSEA VALE RAILWAY
Llansamlet
Tel: 01792 461000

SWINDON AND CRICKLADE STEAM RAILWAY
Blunsdon
Wiltshire
Tel: 01793 771615

TANFIELD RAILWAY
Old Marley Hill
Gateshead
Tyne and Wear
Tel: 0191 388 7545

TELFORD STEAM RAILWAY
Horsehay
Shropshire
Tel: 01952 503880

VALE OF GLAMORGAN RAILWAY
Barry Island
Tel: 01446 748816

WEST SOMERSET RAILWAY
The Station
Minehead
Somerset
Talking timetable: 01643 707650
General: 01643 704996

G.W.R. Prairie tank No. 4141 (built 1946 at Swindon) prepares to move to the other end of the train. No. 4141 in the livery of BR green, is on a special visit to Llangollen Station in 1999.

Left: **On the 23rd May 1999, A4 Class No. 60007 bursts out of the Hadley Wood tunnel. The train is on a special main line running to commemorate the 40th anniversary of the engine's post war speed record of 112mph. Which was achieved over the Stoke bank.**

'Winston Churchill', leaving Ropley with the 12.50 service to Alresford on the Mid Hants Railway on the 22nd July 1995.

Index

A1(3) Class locomotive
36
A4 Class locomotive 35,
36, 37, 39, 78, 79,
156
Aberdeen 36, 108
Agutter, Jenny 14
Alresford 48, 50, 52
Alton 48, 49, 50, 51
Andrew Barclay Co. 12,
108, 110
Arley 78
Ashburton 80
Atlantic Coast Express
89
Auto-train 82, 83, 84,
85, 138, 139
Awdry, Rev. W. 34, 39

B12 engine 10, 11, 12,
13
'Bahamas' engine 16, 20,
35
Barry Condition 36, 120
Barry Scrapyard 24, 26,
50, 146, 147
Battle of Britain Class
35, 36, 38, 51, 55,
56, 57, 59
Beattie tank 84
Beeching, Dr. 80
Beeching Report 6, 48,
49, 54, 74
Beet, Peter 142
'Bellerophon' engine 16,
19, 21
Berwyn 40, 43
Berwyn bank 40, 46
Bewdley 75, 76
'Birch Grove' engine
127, 129
Birkhill 106, 107, 113
Birmingham Railway
Museum 148
Bishops Lydeard 28, 31,

32, 33
Black Five locomotive
30, 63, 72, 87, 95,
146, 148
Blue Anchor 28
Bluebell Railway 22, 27
Bodiam Castle 103
Bodiam station 101
Bo-Peep tunnel 61
Bo'ness & Kinneil
Railway 106, 113
Bo'ness 106, 108, 109,
110, 111, 112
Bo'ness Museum 107,
111, 112
'Boscastle' engine 93, 97
'Bradley Manor' engine
79
Bridgnorth 74, 75, 79
Brighton 79
Brighton Belle 10
British Railways (BR)
17, 22, 26, 28, 35,
41, 42, 48, 49, 62,
74, 78, 81, 86, 90,
93, 101
British Standard Types
44
BS Standard Class 4, 17,
33, 47,
BS Standard Class 4MT
79, 82, 131, 135
BS Standard Class 2 2,
19, 25
BS Standard Class 5 51
BS Standard Class 7100
29
BS Standard 9F 24, 25,
26, 147, 148
Bristol 30, 136
Broad gauge lines 136,
139
Broadway 114, 115
Brunel, I. K. 80
Buckingham Railway

Centre 120–3,
147
Buckfastleigh 80, 81, 82,
83, 84, 85, 87
Bulleid, O.V. 25, 26, 36,
55, 149
Bulleid Pacifics 35,
36, 38, 51, 55, 56,
57, 59, 64, 66, 93,
94, 97
Bury 68, 69, 70, 71, 72,
73
Butterley 130, 131, 132

'Caerphilly Castle'
engine 137, 140
'Calbourne' engine 125,
127
Caledonian Railway
106, 108
Caley tank 108
Cambrian Coast Express
41
'Canadian Pacific'
engine 35, 93
Carnforth Steam
Museum 142, 143
Carrog 40, 42
'Castell Dinas Bran'
engine 45, 47
Castle Class locomotive
20, 52, 87, 116,
137, 138, 140
Cheltenham 114, 115
Churchward, G.J. 90,
116, 136, 149
Churston 86, 88, 91
'Clan Line' engine 139
Class 20 diesel 21, 46
Class 25 diesel 62
Class 40 diesel 35
'Clun Castle' engine
118, 119
Coal tank 18, 21
Collett, Charles 20, 83

Colonel Stephens 100,
101, 103
Corfe Castle 54, 55, 57
Cornish Reviera Express
89
Coronation Scot 36
Corwen 40, 41, 42
Crewe 24, 52, 69
Crowcombe Heathfield
28
'Cumbria' engine 143,
145

Damens 14, 15
'Dame Vera Lynn' engine
62, 66
Darlington 35
Dartmouth 86, 88, 89
Dartmouth (Britannia)
Naval College 88, 89
Dart Valley Railway 80,
81, 91
Dart, River 80, 84, 86,
88
Darlington 65
Dean Forest Railway 83
Dee, River 40
'Defiant' engine 52
'Devon Belle'
observation coach 87,
89, 90
Devonshire bank 30
Didcot Railway Centre
120, 136–141
Didcot Parkway 136
Disabled passengers 33
Doncaster 35, 36, 42
'Duchess of Hamilton'
engine 96
Duchess of Kent 61
'Duchess of Sutherland'
engine 132, 134
Dugaid Drummond class
55, 56, 59
'Duke of Gloucester'

engine 28, 72
'Dumbleton Hall' engine
    81, 82, 87
Dunster 28

'Earl Bathurst' engine
    137, 140, 141
East Coast route 36
Eastern Region 10, 149
East Lancashire Railway
    7, 50, 68
East Grinstead 22, 23,
    24
Edinburgh 36, 37, 42
Edinburgh & Glasgow
    Railway 106, 107
English Tourist Board 48
'Eric Treacy' engine 63
'Errol Lonsdale' engine
    81, 84, 85
Euston station 36
Evercreech Junction 28

Fen Bog 61
Ferry Meadows 34
'Flying Scotsman' engine
    36, 42
Flying Scotsman 36,
    64, 116
Fowler, Henry 30, 32, 79
'Foxcote Manor' engine
    41
'Franklin D. Roosevelt'
    engine 50, 52
French Railways 38
'Freshwater' engine 127
Frome 30, 136, 139
Furness Railway 142,
    143, 144

Germany 34, 38, 39
Glasgow 35, 106, 107,
    108
Glasgow Museum of
    Transport 109
Gloucestershire
    Warwickshire Railway
    114–19
Glyndyfrdwy 40, 41
Goathland 60, 62, 64,
    65, 67
'Goliath' engine 88, 90,
    91
Goodrington Sands 86,
    87, 91
Gotherington 115
Great Central Railway
    92–9

Great Central – Original
    railway 99, 120,
    123
'Great Marquess' (The)
    engine 35, 39
Great Northern Railway
    35, 36
Great Western Railway
    (GWR) 28, 30,
    33, 41, 74, 76, 79,
    80, 82, 85, 86, 88,
    89, 90, 114, 115,
    116, 120, 136,
    138, 141, 147,
    146, 147, 149, 149
'Green Arrow' engine
    140, 141
Greek Railway's 49, 50
Greet tunnel 115
Gresley, Sir Nigel 9, 12,
    35, 36, 37, 132
Gresley coaches 12, 75
Grosmont 60, 63, 65, 67
Grouping 36, 69, 149

Hall Class locomotive
    87, 96, 141
Hampton Loade 75
Harmans Cross 54
'Hartland' engine 64, 66
Harvey, Bill 10, 11
Hastings 61, 100
Havenstreet 124, 126,
    127, 128
Haverthwaite 142, 143
Haworth 14, 18, 19
Haydock Foundry 16,
    17, 19
Henschell & Co. 38
Heywood 68, 70
Highland Railway 108
'Hinderton Hall' 141
Holt 8, 9
Holt Flyer 8, 13
Horsted Keynes 22, 23,
    26, 27
Hudswell Clarke 34, 39
Hunslet Austerity tank
    11, 13, 81, 82,
    115, 143, 144
Hyde Park Works 62,
    108
Hymek, diesel 72

Ingrow 14, 15, 18
Ingrow Carriage museum
    15, 21
Irwell Valley 68

Island Line 124
Isle of Wight Steam
    Railway 124–9
Ivatt, H. G. 70, 149
Ivatt Mogul 69, 70, 71,
    73, 104, 105
Ivatt 2-6-2T tank 52

James the Red Engine
    52, 53
Jinty 0-6-0 tank 41, 45
Jubilee Class locomotives
    16, 20, 97, 98

K4 Class 35, 39
Keighley & Worth
    Valley Railway
    14–21
Kelling Camp Halt 8
'Kelton Fell' engine 112
Kent & East Sussex
    Railway 100–5
Kidderminster 74, 75,
    76, 77
King Arthur Class 25
King Class locomotive
    87, 138, 140, 158
'King Edward I' engine
    120, 140, 158
Kinneil 106
Kingscote 22, 23, 24
Kings Cross station 36,
    42, 130
Kingswear 86, 88, 89, 91
Kinnaber Junction 36,
    108
'Kolhapur' engine 20,
    97, 98

'Lady Victoria' engine
    110
Lakeside &
Haverthwaite Railway
    142–5
Leeds 14
Leicester North station
    92, 93, 96
Levisham 62
Light Railway Order 6,
    41, 50
Light Railway's 102
Little 0-4-0T shunting
    engines 122, 135
Llangollen 40, 41, 42,
    43, 45, 157
Llangollen Railway
    40–7, 50
'Locomotion' engine 35,

36
London 36, 37, 48, 61,
    69, 86, 89, 100
London Midland
Scottish Railway, (LMS)
    17, 30, 41, 70, 93,
    94, 102, 132, 149
London & North
Eastern Railway (LNER)
    9, 93, 107, 132,
    141, 144, 149
London Brighton &
South Coast Railway
    100
Longmoor Military
    Railway 50, 62, 85
Loughborough 92, 93,
    94, 97, 98
Low's Crossing 106, 110

Maher, Austin 142
Manchester 30
Manor Class locomotive
    33, 41, 79,
Manuel 106
'Maude' engine 109, 111
Maunsell, R.E.L. 25, 52,
    120
Mechanical horse 77
Medstead & Four Marks
    48, 50
Merchant Navy Class
    55, 93, 139
Metropolitan Railway
    18, 120
Metro Trains 14, 70
Mid-Hants Railway 48–
    53, 70
Middleton Railway 22
Midford 30, 31, 32
Midland Railway 14, 15,
    30, 130
Midland Region 69, 95
Midland Railway Centre
    130–5, 141
Midlands & Gt.
Northern Joint Railway
    9, 12, 149
Minehead 28, 29, 30,
    32, 33
Mountfield tunnel 61

N Class (SR) 52
National Railway
Museum see National
    Collection
National Collection 26,
    65, 84

Neilsons Works 112
Nene Valley Railway 34–9
Nene, River 34, 38
Newby Bridge 145
'Newport' engine 126
No. 20 engine 144, 145
No. 101A engine 37
Norden 54, 59
Nord Railways 38
North British Railway Co. 107, 108, 109
Northiam 101
North Norfolk Railway 8–13
North York Moors Railway 50, 60–7
Norton Fitzwarren 28
'Norwegian' engine 104, 105
Nottingham Heritage Centre 92

Oakworth 14, 15 20
'Odney Manor' engine 33
Old Kirk Church 109, 110
Orton Mere 34
Oxenhope 14, 15

P Class locomotive 101, 105
Paddington Station 86, 89
Paignton 81, 86, 87, 88, 89, 90, 91
Paignton & Dartmouth Steam Railway 86–91
Pannier tanks 21, 41, 43, 110, 122, 123
Peterborough 10, 34, 35, 36, 39
Peterborough Development Corporation 34
Peters, Ivo 30
Pickering 61, 65
Pines Express 24, 30
'Pioneer' train 23, 27
Platform ticket machine 102
Poland 34
Polish State Railway's 34, 39, 49
Prairie tank 31, 83, 84, 85, 118, 146, 157,

158
'Princess Margaret Rose' engine 130, 132, 133, 134
Princess Royal Class 96, 130, 132, 133

Q Class locomotive 25, 26, 27
Quainton Road 120, 122, 123
Queens Park Works 16
Quorn & Woodhouse 92

Races to the north 36, 108
Radstock 30, 136, 137
Railtrack 28, 68
Railway Children, The film 14, 15, 16
Ramsbottom 69, 70, 71, 73
Rawtenstall 70, 71, 73
'Repton' engine 61, 63
Riddles, R.A. 24, 62
'Ring Haw' engine 10, 11
'Robert Nelson' engine 118
Robertsbridge station 101, 103
Rolvenden 101, 103, 105
Ropley 48, 50, 51, 53
Rothley 92, 95
Ryde 124

S15 Class locomotive 27
S160 locomotives 49, 50, 52, 67
'Sapper' engine 81, 82
Saxa Salt wagon 111
Schools Class locomotives 25, 61, 63
Scotland 16, 36, 69
Scottish Railway's 108
Severn Valley Railway 39, 74–9
Sheffield Park 22, 23, 24, 25, 26, 27
Shepherd, David 24
Sheringham 8, 10, 11, 13
Shrewsbury 42
'Sir Nigel Gresley' engine 35, 37, 39, 156

'Sir Robert Peel' engine 115, 117
Smallbrook Junction 124, 125, 126, 128, 129
Somersault signals 35
Somerset & Dorset Joint Railway 9, 10, 24, 28, 30, 31, 32, 149
South African Railways 121
South Devon Railway 80–5
South Eastern & Chatham Railway 22, 23, 24, 25, 27, 100
Southern Railway 10, 25, 48, 64, 86, 87, 90, 124, 126
Standard Class, see British Standard Types
Stanier 8F engine 17, 18, 21, 36, 93, 94, 96, 98
Stanier, William 16, 20, 79, 96
Staverton 80, 82, 84
Steam on the Met 79, 120, 122
Steamtown, USA 56
Stephenson, George 60, 61, 65, 67
Stirling 01 Class 25
Stockton & Darlington Railway 83, 144
Stogumber 28
Stratford-upon-Avon 10, 114, 115
'Stepney' engine 22
Stroudley Terriers 22, 100, 104, 105, 124, 126, 129
Swanage 54, 56, 58
Swanage Railway 54–9
Swanswick Junction 130
Sweden 34, 105
Swedish Railways 37, 39
Swindon 24, 41

Taunton 28, 32, 89
Tenterden 100, 102, 103, 104, 105
'The Diana' diesel 62
Thomas the Tank Engine 6, 34, 42,

45, 46, 53, 114, 117, 118
'Tiny' engine 81, 85
Toddington 114, 115, 118, 119
Torbay 86
Torbay Express 86, 88, 89
Totnes 80, 81

'Union of South Africa' engine 78, 79
United States of America 50, 56

VE50 7, 51, 93, 96

Wansford 34, 35, 37, 38
Wareham 54
War Department 24
Washford 28, 30, 32
Watercress Line, see Mid-Hants Railway
Waterloo Station 55, 56, 86, 89
WD Austerity Locomotives 17, 62, 63, 66, 67, 81, 143, 144
West Coast route 36
West Country Class 30, 51, 64, 93, 97
Western Region 79
'Western Statesman' diesel 72
West Somerset Railway 28–33
Weybourne 8, 11, 12, 13
Williton 28, 30, 32
Winchcombe 114
Winchcombe Railway Museum 117
Windermere, Lake 142, 143
'Winston Churchill' engine 51, 157
'Witherslack Hall' engine 96
Wittersham Road station 101
Woodham, Dai 6, 34, 55, 79, 90, 146–8
Worth Valley Railway – see Keighley
Yanks film 14
Yarwell Junction 34